A Basic Guide to

EVIDENCE
IN
CRIMINAL CASES

Third Edition

A Basic Guide to
EVIDENCE
IN
CRIMINAL CASES
Third Edition

The Honourable
Roger E. Salhany

CARSWELL
Thomson Professional Publishing

The publisher is not engaged in rendering legal, accounting or other professional advice. If legal advice or other expert assistance is required, the services of a competent professional should be sought. The analysis contained herein represents the opinions of the authors and should in no way be construed as being either official or unofficial policy of any governmental body.

Canadian Cataloguing in Publication Data

Salhany, Roger E.
  A basic guide to evidence in criminal cases

3rd ed.
Includes index.
ISBN 0-459-55273-2 (bound). — ISBN 0-459-55275-9 (pbk.).

1. Evidence, Criminal – Canada. I. Title.

KE9312.S35 1994   345.71'06   C94-932760-3
KF8935.ZA2S35 1994

∞ The acid-free paper used in this publication meets the minimum requirements of American National Standard for Information Sciences – Permanence of Paper for Printed Library Materials, ANSI Z39.48-1984.

CARSWELL
Thomson Professional Publishing

One Corporate Plaza, 2075 Kennedy Road, Scarborough, Ontario M1T 3V4
Customer Service:
Toronto 1-416-609-3800
Elsewhere in Canada/U.S. 1-800-387-5164
Fax 1-416-298-5094

To my wife Terri

Preface to the First Edition

Trying to learn the law of evidence is like trying to learn a new language. For every rule there is usually an exception, and for each exception there is often an additional exception. This is probably because what the rules of evidence seek to achieve is a delicate balance between probity and fairness. However, when we look more closely, we discover that too often the rules or exceptions are based on historical anachronisms or public policy rather than common sense.

This book purports to be nothing more than its title suggests. It is a guide, not a text book. Its purpose is to explain not only what kinds of evidence are permitted in a criminal trial but, more importantly, why certain rules exclude evidence that common sense tells us might assist in the discovery of the truth. It is offered to police officers, social workers, investigators, law students and anyone interested in understanding what goes on in the court room.

I want to express my gratitude to my venerable colleague, Judge Costello who kindly shared his experience of thirty years as a trial judge, and to Professor Syd Usprich for his many scholarly suggestions and grammatical corrections, Once more, I want to thank Irene Parker who found time in her very busy schedule to type the manuscript.

New Dundee, July 23, 1990   R.E.S.

Preface to the Second Edition

Although this book was written initially as a primer for police officers, law students and others trying to understand the complicated world of criminal evidence, many lawyers and judges told me that they found it valuable as a refresher course and requested that I update regularly. For that reason, I have decided to expand this edition to cover a number of new areas in each chapter as well as to discuss the implications of such important recent decisions as *Gruenke, Khan, C. (M.H.)* and *Hebert*.

New Dundee, January 29, 1992   R.E.S.

Preface to the Third Edition

This edition brings up to date the many judicial developments in criminal evidence in the last three years. Some of those developments involve the testimony of children (*Marquand*), prior inconsistent statements (*K.C.B.*), previous consistent statements (*F.(J.E.)*), the use of expert testimony to explain human behaviour (*Burns*) and the admissibility of an expert's opinion as to disposition (*Mohan*), just to name a few.

Chapters 1 and 8 have also been expanded in a number of areas.

I am grateful to two of my colleagues, Mr. Justice Stephen Glithero and Mr. Justice Robert Reilly who offered many valuable suggestions. Any errors in the text are mine.

New Dundee, November 24, 1994   R.E.S.

Table of Contents

Table of Cases

PART A

Admissibility

1

General Principles

1. INTRODUCTION

In every criminal case, there are three things that the Crown must establish in order to succeed in proving its case. The first is that a crime was committed or what lawyers call the "*actus reus*". The second thing is that the accused standing in the prisoner's dock committed the crime or what is known as identity. The third and final thing that must be established is that the accused intended to commit the crime, in the sense that it was his deliberate act, or in some cases, there was recklessness or gross negligence. This is what is called the "*mens rea*". However, intention is not to be confused with motive because why a person commits a crime is not really something that the court concerns itself with, although it may be relevant in some instances, as a matter of circumstantial evidence, to prove one of the three issues. There are also certain crimes where intention is not relevant; sometimes the person may not even be aware that he was committing the crime. These are called strict liability offences and are not necessary to this discussion.

Proof of an issue may be made either by way of direct evidence or circumstantial evidence. Direct evidence is simply evidence that directly proves a fact in issue. If the issue is whether A walked across the street, B may give evidence that he saw A walk cross the street and such evidence is direct evidence. Circumstantial evidence is evidence of surrounding circumstances from which an inference may be drawn by the trier that a certain fact occurred. B may not have seen A walk across the street but he may have seen him on one side of the street one minute and then on the other side a minute later. Circumstantial evidence allows the trier of fact to draw the inference that a fact occurred provided that the inference is a reasonable one.

Therefore, the first question that a lawyer involved in the case, whether the prosecutor or the defence counsel, must ask himself is this: what does a particular piece of evidence go to prove? This is the very question that police officers must ask themselves when called upon to investigate a crime after arrival at the scene. As the officer looks over the crime scene, he or she will make a number of observations. Items will be seen that arouse suspicion such as weapons, broken windows, footprints, or injured parties. Persons may come forward and give a statement about their observations. The officer will be advised of certain information and will conduct an investigation that may turn up objects or statements that may or may not be relevant to the case. The officer must continually keep in mind the question: what does this go to prove?

2. TEST OF RELEVANCY

As has been already noted, there are three issues that the Crown must prove in every criminal case: the act, the identity and the intent. With these three issues of proof (and those issues alone), we can formulate a rule or test of admissibility. That rule is simply this: evidence is admissible if it is relevant to one of those three issues. To put it another way, the relevance of any piece of evidence must be determined only in relation to the issues that the prosecution must establish.[1] If the evidence is logically probative of one of those issues, then it is said to be relevant and admissible so long as it is not contrary to one of the rules that may exclude evidence which will be discussed in the next two sections. What is relevant will generally be decided by logic and human experience. In *Corbett*[2] Mr. Justice LaForest described the rule this way,

> All relevant evidence is admissible, subject to a discretion to exclude matters that may unduly prejudice, mislead or confuse the trier of fact, take up too much time, or that should otherwise be excluded on clear grounds of law or policy. Questions of relevancy and exclusion are, of course,

---

[1] *Cloutier* (1979), 12 C.R. (3d) 10, 48 C.C.C. (2d) 1 (S.C.C.)

[2] (1988), 64 C.R. (3d) 1, 41 C.C.C. (3d) 385 (S.C.C.), at pp. 33-34 (C.R.).

matters for the trial judge, but over the years many specific exclusionary rules have been developed for the guidance of the trial judge, so much so that the law of evidence may superficially appear to consist simply of a series of exceptions to the rules of admissibility, with exceptions to the exceptions, and their subexceptions.

Although, evidence to be relevant and admissible must be logically probative of one of the three issues, there is no requirement that it must go directly to the proof of one of those issues. As Mr. Justice Doherty pointed out in *P.(R.)*,[3]

> Evidence may, however, be relevant even though it does not go directly to the proof of a material fact, or even alone provide the basis for an inference that the material fact exists. Evidence may be relevant by its combination with other evidence adduced in the case. Such is the essence of circumstantial evidence.

This means that where evidence offered by one side is circumstantial in nature, the trial judge is required to examine that evidence in the light of all of the factual issues that are raised in the case. Although generally, relevance will depend on the ultimate issue in the case (whether it be the act, identity or intent or all three), the evidence, although not directly relevant to one of those issues, may be relevant to another factor which is relevant to one of those issues.

Unfortunately, even the courts often have difficulty in deciding what is relevant to a fact in issue when it comes to circumstantial evidence. For example in *Cloutier*,[4] the accused was charged with importing marijuana. Marijuana had been found concealed in a piece of furniture (a dresser) imported into Canada and stored at the home of the accused's mother on his instructions. The trial judge had refused to admit certain items found by the police during a search of the accused's home. These included a glass jar containing a green substance analyzed as marijuana and certificates of analysis of a cigarette butt made of marijuana and traces of marijuana found on scales and pipes in the premises. A majority panel of the Supreme Court of Canada held that the trial judge was correct in his ruling. The majority said that the fact the accused used marijuana did not create a logical inference that he knew or ought to have known that the dresser contained a narcotic at the time it

---

[3] (1990), 58 C.C.C. (3d) 334 (Ont. H.C.), at pp. 339-340.
[4] *Supra*, note 1.

was imported. All it showed was that a user of a narcotic was more likely to import the substance illegally than a non-user. Nor could the evidence be used to prove motive since it did not "disclose a sufficiently close logical connection between the facts that are to be proven as a motive and the crime committed." The minority panel came to the exact opposite conclusion. They concluded that since guilty intent cannot be established by direct evidence in such cases, it is "necessary to admit in evidence every bit of circumstantial evidence." There was a clear connection between the fact that the accused was a user of a prohibited narcotic and the presence of that narcotic concealed in the dresser. So long as there was some connection, even though not conclusive, the evidence had to be admitted for what it was worth. Moreover, if the accused was a marijuana user, then his motive in importing it was obvious.

A little over four years later, a majority panel of the Supreme Court came to the opposite conclusion on a similar fact situation. In *Morris*[5] the accused and several others were charged with conspiracy to import and traffic in heroin from Hong Kong. The Crown's case was based on surveillance and wiretap evidence. When the accused was arrested, a newspaper article headed "The Heroin Trade Moves to Pakistan" and written two years prior to the offence was found in the accused's apartment. This time the majority held that an inference could be drawn from the presence of the newspaper article in the accused's apartment that he had informed himself on the sources of supply of heroin, a subject of vital interest to an importer of heroin. It raised the inference that the accused had taken preparatory steps to import heroin or had contemplated it, even though the article referred to the heroin trade in Pakistan and not Hong Kong. The minority panel of the Court, relying on *Cloutier*,[6] held that the sole relevancy of the evidence was to show that it was more likely that persons who are traffickers keep such information than people who do not. Since such evidence only went to the disposition of the accused to commit the offence, it should not have been admitted by the trial judge.

---

[5] (1984), 36 C.R. (3d) 1, 7 C.C.C. (3d) 97 (S.C.C.).
[6] *Supra*, note 1.

3. JUDICIAL DISCRETION TO EXCLUDE EVIDENCE

The general rule at common law was that apart from the question of confessions, the court was not concerned with how evidence was obtained. So long as the evidence was relevant to a fact in issue, the court allowed the evidence to be admitted.

In the last fifty years, however, Canadian and British courts have become concerned about whether trial judges have and should have a discretion to exclude evidence which is otherwise admissible, where it would operate unfairly to the accused. In *Wray*,[7] the Supreme Court of Canada grudgingly indicated that it was prepared to recognize a limited judicial discretion to exclude evidence, but only where that evidence had little probative value and was so gravely prejudicial to the accused that it would prevent a fair trial.

Since the *Wray* case, Canadian courts have struggled over the extent of a judge's discretion to exclude evidence. Unfortunately, even the Supreme Court has been divided on the issue. That difference in views was summed up by Mr. Justice La Forest in *Potvin*[8] in these words,

> As my colleague notes, some have interpreted Martland J.'s dictum (in *Wray*) as limiting the discretion solely to situations where the evidence is highly prejudicial to the accused and is of only modest value. I do not accept this restrictive approach to the discretion... under English law a judge in a criminal trial always has a discretion to exclude evidence if, in the judge's opinion, its prejudicial effect substantially outweighs its probative value... The discretion is grounded in the judge's duty to ensure a fair trial.

Nevertheless, more recently Madame Justice McLachlin delivering the majority judgment in *Seaboyer*,[9] regarded the *Wray* formula as superceded by the more expansive formula expressed by LaForest in *Potvin* and that "admissibility will depend upon the probative effect of the evidence balanced against the prejudice caused to the accused by its admission"[10]

There are some instances where the right to exclude evidence which is highly prejudicial has been specifically recognized. One was the *Potvin* case dealing with section 715 of the *Criminal Code*.[11]

---

[7] 11 C.R.N.S. 235, [1970] 4 C.C.C. 1 (S.C.C.).

[8] (1989), 68 C.R. (3d) 193, 47 C.C.C. (3d) 289 (S.C.C.), at p. 243 (C.R.).

[9] (1991), 7 C.R. (4th) 117, 66 C.C.C. (3d) 321 (S.C.C.).

[10] *Sweitzer* (1982), 29 C.R. (3d) 97, 68 C.C.C. (2d) 193 (S.C.C.), at p. 196 (C.C.C.).

[11] R.S.C. 1985, c. C-46.

Section 715 allows the Crown to read in at trial evidence given by a witness at the accused's preliminary hearing or at a previous trial on the same charge who now refuses to give evidence or to be sworn, or is dead, insane, too ill to travel or testify, or is absent from Canada. Section 715 also provides that the trial judge may refuse to permit the evidence to be read in if the accused satisfies him that he did not have full opportunity to cross-examine the witness. Madame Justice Wilson described how that discretion should be exercised by the trial judge,[12]

> In my view there are two main types of mischief at which the discretion (to refuse to admit evidence under section 715) might be aimed. First, the discretion could be aimed at situations in which there has been unfairness in the manner in which the evidence was obtained... An example of unfairness in obtaining the testimony might be a case in which, although the witness was temporarily absent from Canada, the Crown could have obtained the witness's attendance at trial with a minimal degree of effort. Another example might be a case in which the Crown was aware at the time when the evidence was initially taken that the witness would not be available to testify at the trial but did not inform the accused of the fact so that he could make best use of the opportunity to cross-examine the witness at the earlier proceeding... A different concern at which the discretion might have been aimed is the effect of the admission of the previously-taken evidence on the fairness of the trial itself. This concern flows from the principle of the law of evidence that evidence may be excluded if it is highly prejudicial to the accused and of only modest probative value...

Another instance where the Supreme Court has held that there is a discretion to exclude evidence that may be probative but also gravely prejudicial is where the Crown seeks to cross-examine the accused or a witness under section 12 of the *Canada Evidence Act*[13] on his criminal record. Section 12 of the Act permits the accused or a witness to be asked whether he has been convicted of any offence and, if he denies or refuses to answer the question, allows the record to be proved. In *Corbett*[14] the Supreme Court held that the trial judge has a limited discretion to prevent cross-examination on a previous criminal record where it might unduly prejudice, mislead or confuse the trier of fact.

---

[12] *Potvin, supra*, note 8 at p. 237 (C.R.).
[13] R.S.C. 1985, c. C-5.
[14] *Supra*, note 2.

4. CONSTITUTIONAL REQUIREMENT TO EXCLUDE EVIDENCE

The *Charter of Rights and Freedoms*[15] enacted in 1982, has substantially broadened the court's powers to exclude evidence where a right or freedom guaranteed by the *Charter* has been denied or infringed. Section 24 provides,

> 24(1) Anyone whose rights or freedoms, as guaranteed by this Charter, have been infringed or denied may apply to a court of competent jurisdiction to obtain such remedy as the court considers appropriate and just in the circumstances.
>
> (2) Where, in proceedings under subsection (1), a court concludes that evidence was obtained in a manner that infringed or denied any rights or freedoms guaranteed by this Charter, *the evidence shall be excluded* if it is established that, having regard to all the circumstances, the admission of it in the proceedings would bring the administration of justice into disrepute.

It is important to note that section 24(2) is concerned not only with the fairness of an accused's trial, but also with the method by which the evidence was obtained by the prosecution. For example, in *Manninen*,[16] the accused told a police officer that he did not want to say anything until he had seen his lawyer. However, the police officer continued to question him and obtained an incriminating answer which the trial judge relied upon in convicting the accused. It was held that the officer's conduct was a deliberate and flagrant disregard of the accused's right to counsel as guaranteed by section 10(b) of the *Charter*.

But section 24(2) does not say that every breach of the *Charter* will result in the exclusion of evidence obtained by that breach. It is only where it is established by the accused that "having regard to all the circumstances, the admission of it in the proceedings would ["could " i.e "susceptible" under the French version] bring the administration of justice into disrepute". In *Collins*[17] the Supreme Court of Canada ruled that there are three factors that a trial judge should consider in determining whether the administration of justice would [could] be brought into disrepute. The first is whether

---

[15] *The Canadian Charter of Rights and Freedoms*, Part 1 of the Constitution Act, 1982, being schedule B to the Canada Act 1982 (U.K.), 1982, c. 11.

[16] (1987), 58 C.R. (3d) 97, 34 C.C.C. (3d) 385 (S.C.C.).

[17] (1987), 56 C.R. (3d) 193, 33 C.C.C. (3d) 1 (S.C.C.).

the admission of the evidence will affect the fairness of the trial. Here the Court drew a distinction between evidence that was already pre-existing, such as a murder weapon, and evidence which was obtained purely as a result of a *Charter* violation, such as a confession. A *Charter* violation relating to pre-existing evidence was not as serious as one where the evidence was obtained after a violation of the *Charter* because the use of such evidence, such as a person's confession, strikes at one of the fundamental tenets of a fair trial, the right against self-incrimination. The Court said that in the case of pre-existing evidence, the more serious the offence, the less likely the evidence would be excluded, as that, in itself, would [could] bring the administration of justice into disrepute. On the other hand, where the evidence was obtained as a result of a *Charter* violation, the more serious the offence, the more damaging to the system's repute would be an unfair trial, in which case the evidence should be excluded.

The second factor which the Supreme Court said that a trial judge must consider is the seriousness of the violation. Relevant to this issue is whether the violation was committed in good faith, whether it was inadvertent or of a merely technical nature, whether it was motivated by urgency or to prevent the loss of evidence, and whether the evidence could have been obtained without a *Charter* violation.

The last factor which the Court said that the judge should consider is the effect excluding the evidence would have on the administration of justice. Here the focus again is on the fairness of the trial. Even where the breach was trivial, the charge serious and the evidence essential to substantiate the charge, the evidence would not automatically be admissible particularly where it would result in an unfair trial.

Lamer J. (now C.J.C.) wrote,[18]

Real evidence that was obtained in a manner that violated the Charter will rarely operate unfairly for that reason alone. The real evidence existed irrespective of the violation of the Charter and its use does not render the trial unfair. However, the situation is very different with respect to cases where, after a violation of the Charter, the accused is conscripted against himself through a confession or other evidence emanating from him. *The use of such evidence would render the trial unfair, for it did not exist prior*

---

[18] *Ibid.*, p. 211 (C.R.).

*to the violation and strikes at one of the fundamental tenets of a fair trial,
the right against self-incrimination.* [Emphasis added]

In two subsequent decisions of the same Court, *Elshaw*[19] and
Broyles,[20] it was stressed that where the tainted evidence affects the
fairness of the trial, the second set of factors, that is, good faith
on the part of the police, cannot reduce the seriousness of the violation. This means that evidence affecting the fairness of a trial will
normally be excluded as the rule rather than as the exception.

5. ADMISSIBILITY VERSUS WEIGHT

It is important to draw a distinction between the admissibility
of evidence and its weight. When one side seeks to introduce evidence and the other side objects, the trial judge must rule as to its
admissibility. That decision involves a question of law which only
the trial judge can decide. If the trial judge rules that the evidence
is admissible, then the question of what weight should be attached
to the evidence is a question solely for the trier of fact, whether
that is the judge sitting alone or a jury.

This distinction is of particular importance when we come to
Chapter 3 dealing with hearsay evidence and recent developments
which authorize a trial judge to admit hearsay which meets the twin
test of necessity and reliability. Whenever such evidence is admitted, the trial judge must remind the jury (or himself where he sits
alone) of the potential unreliability of such evidence and instruct
them that the question of the weight to be attached to such evidence is for them alone to determine.

---

[19] (1992), 7 C.R. (4th) 333, 67 C.C.C. (3d) 97 (S.C.C.).
[20] (1992), 7 C.R. (4th) 1 (S.C.C.).

2

Kinds of Evidence

1. INTRODUCTION

The law recognizes two methods of proof: direct evidence and circumstantial evidence. There is no particular magic in these terms. Direct evidence is simply evidence that directly proves a fact in issue.

For example, if the fact in issue is whether Smith stabbed Jones, a witness who testifies that he saw Smith stab Jones is giving what is known as direct evidence.

Circumstantial evidence, on the other hand, is evidence of surrounding circumstances from which an inference may be drawn that a certain fact occurred. Let us take our previous example of Smith and Jones and let us assume that the witness did not see Smith stab Jones. Instead, he observed Smith walking down the street all covered in blood with a knife in his hand and saw Jones, a short distance away, lying in a pool of blood. Although the witness did not see Smith stab Jones, it is reasonable to infer from all of the surrounding circumstances that Smith did in fact do so. This is what is known as circumstantial evidence as opposed to direct evidence of a fact in issue.

Although both kinds of evidence are admissible, the court scrutinizes circumstantial evidence more carefully. The burden of proof will be discussed in a subsequent chapter. It is only necessary to say at this stage that the burden of proof is upon the Crown to prove the guilt of an accused and such proof must be established beyond a reasonable doubt. Where proof is based upon circumstantial evidence either in whole or in part, a judge will usually caution a jury (or himself or herself when trying the case alone) that before they can rely on circumstantial evidence, they must be satisfied that the guilt of the accused is the only logical inference to be drawn from such evidence.

There are three kinds of evidence that are generally recognized as admissible to establish a fact in issue. They are: oral testimony or viva voce evidence; real evidence which includes documents or things such as weapons, etc; and demonstrative evidence which includes photographs, maps, etc.

2. ORAL TESTIMONY

(a) Generally

The most common way that evidence is given is by a witness entering the witness box and testifying in open court. In Canada, as well as throughout other common-law jurisdictions, the order of questioning a witness is strictly controlled. The witness is first examined by the side who calls him; he may then be cross-examined by the other side; and finally he may be re-examined by the first side. Unlike the continental system, which allows a witness to repeat his evidence with little interruption, the evidence of a witness is tightly controlled by the questions asked. This does not mean that the witness must answer either yes or no. However, the witness is expected to be responsive to the questions put to him. He is not entitled to make a speech unconnected with that question.

There is a distinction, however, between the type of questions that may be asked in chief (that is by the person who calls the witness) and the questions that may be asked in cross-examination (that is by the person who is on the other side). When a witness is examined in chief, the examiner must not lead him nor suggest the answer to him except on matters that are not disputed or not in issue. For example, a witness may be led on all preliminary background matters such as his age, marital status, children and occupation, unless those issues are disputed. Often a judge will permit the examiner to lead a witness of tender years or who is intellectually challenged and is having difficulty expressing himself. Such evidence will generally not be given the same weight as evidence which is not led.

On the other hand, cross-examination may suggest answers to the witness. The purpose of cross-examination is to test the accuracy of what the witness has said in chief. It is also to bring out new evidence that the witness did not give in chief. Once cross-examination is completed, the side that called the witness is entitled to re-examine him. Re-examination is restricted solely to matters that were raised in cross-examination and is only allowed in order to clarify those answers that were given.

(b) Competence of the Witness

(i) Generally

Not everyone is allowed to enter the witness box and give oral evidence. A person called as a witness must be competent to give testimony. Competence refers to the legal qualification of a person to given evidence. Competence must also be distinguished from compellability. Compellability refers to the right of either side of a dispute to call a witness to give evidence and the legal obligation of that witness to testify.

Until the end of the last century, there were a great many individuals who were considered not competent to give evidence. For example, a person might not be allowed to testify because he had an interest in the case and therefore his evidence was not considered reliable. In fact, it was not until 1640 that a person charged with a felony (i.e. a serious crime), was allowed to call witnesses for the defence. And until the end of that century, witnesses for the defence were not allowed to give their evidence under oath. The theory was that such witnesses, if they contradicted the witnesses for the prosecution, were probably lying.

Today, generally all witnesses (subject to the exceptions below) are presumed competent to testify if they understand the nature and obligation of an oath. Until recently, this meant that the proposed witness had to understand the spiritual consequences of an oath. In other words, he or she had to believe in God or a Supreme Being. That requirement is no longer necessary. When a person takes an oath, it means that he understands the moral obligation to tell the truth.[1] The person must also understand the legal consequences of lying, namely, the possible prosecution for perjury. As Madame Justice McLachlin said in *Khan*,[2] "(B)efore a person can give evidence under oath, it must be established that the oath in some way gets a hold on his conscience, that there is an appreciation of the significance of testifying in court under oath."

For a long period, those who would not or could not take an oath because of their religion, or lack of it, were not allowed to testify. In Canada an oath is no longer required. Section 14 of the *Canada Evidence Act*[3] allows someone to affirm if the traditional oath is objected to on the grounds of conscientious scruples or because the person would not be bound by it. In such instance, the person is required to solemnly affirm that the evidence to be given by him "shall be the truth, the whole truth and nothing but the truth." This means that if the witness tells a lie, he is liable to prosecution for perjury just as if he had taken the traditional oath.

Although all witnesses are now presumed competent to testify, a witness may be declared incompetent if he suffers from a condition that renders it unsafe for the trier of fact to rely on his tes-

---

[1] *Fletcher* (1982), 1 C.C.C. (3d) 370 (Ont. C.A.), leave to appeal to S.C.C. refused (1983), 48 N.R. 319 (S.C.C.).
[2] (1990), 79 C.R. (3d) 1, 59 C.C.C. (3d) 92 (S.C.C.), at p. 7 (C.R.).
[3] R.S.C. 1985, c. C-5.

timony. However, a finding that the witness suffers from a particular mental or psychiatric condition does not necessarily or in itself disqualify him to give evidence. In order to disqualify a witness, the court must be satisfied that his particular condition is such as to substantially negative the trustworthiness of his evidence on the specific subject.

The general rule, as we shall see later, is that an expert may not testify as to the credibility of a witness. However, where the opposing side seeks to challenge the competency of a witness because of a particular mental or psychiatric condition, experts are permitted to go further and say that the witness suffers from some "hidden defect" which affects the reliability of the testimony. Moreover, the expert's evidence is not confined to a general opinion about the unreliability of the witness. The expert will be permitted to testify about all of the matters necessary to show not only the foundation of, and the reasons for, the diagnosis but also the extent to which the credibility is affected.[4]

(ii) The Accused

The most serious restriction on the right to testify was on the accused. An accused was not allowed to testify because it was believed that since he or she had an interest in the result, they would probably lie. It was not until 1898, less than a hundred years ago that an accused in England was allowed to give evidence under oath on his own behalf. In Canada, that right was granted a few years earlier. Section 3 of the *Act* specifically provides that "a person is not incompetent to give evidence by reason of interest or crime."

Section 4(1) of the *Act* goes on to provide that "every person charged with an offence is... *a competent witness for the defence*, whether the person so charged is charged solely or jointly with any other person." This means that although an accused is competent to testify in his own defence, he is not competent (and therefore not compellable) at the instance of the prosecution to testify against himself. It also means that a person who is being jointly tried is not competent at the instance of the prosecution to testify against a co-accused (nor compellable at the instance of a co-accused). How-

---

[4] *Hawke* (1975), 29 C.R.N.S. 1, 22 C.C.C. (2d) 19 (Ont. C.A.); *Toohey v. Metropolitan Police Commissioner*, [1965] 1 All E.R. 506 (H.L.).

ever, since the accused is competent to testify on his own behalf, he becomes an ordinary witness once he takes the witness stand to testify in his defence, and is required to answer questions by the prosecution or counsel for a co-accused regarding his involvement in the offence and the involvement of a co-accused.

(iii) The Spouse of the Accused

Another person who was not allowed to give evidence was the spouse of an accused. This was initially based on the theory that husband and wife were one and, if the accused was incompetent to testify, so was his spouse. Eventually, this reason was abandoned and justification for the rule was based on the natural repugnance of using the law to compel a wife to betray her husband or vice versa, if marital harmony was to be preserved. The rule was applied even if the parties were not husband and wife at the time of the offence so long as they were married at the time of the trial.[5] Ironically, the same rule was not applied to prevent a child from betraying a parent, or a sister or brother betraying a sibling.

The rule which rendered a spouse incompetent to testify was abolished in Canada at the end of the last century by section 4 of the *Act*. Section 4(1) now makes a spouse "a competent for the defence" but not for the prosecution except with respect to those offences (generally sexual offences or assault against children) specified in subsections 2 and 4 of section 4, or where the offence charged affects the spouse's health or liberty. Moreover, the courts have indicated that they intend to restrict the rule to the policy considerations underlying it. For example, in *Salituro*[6] the Supreme Court of Canada said that if the parties, although legally married, are separated with no reasonable prospect for reconciliation, then the public policy of promoting marital harmony would have no rational foundation and there could not be spousal incompetence. It has also been said that the time for determining whether the spouses have irreconcilably separated is at the time of the trial.[7] Moreover, the so-called "common law marriage" or "common law relationship" has not been recognized by the courts so as to render one

---

[5] *Hoskyn v. Metro Police Commissioner* (1978), 67 Cr.App.R. 88 (H.L.).

[6] (1990), 78 C.R. (3d) 68, 56 C.C.C. (3d) 350 (Ont. C.A.), approved S.C.C. (1992), 9 C.R. (4th) 324, 68 C.C.C. (3d) 289 (S.C.C.).

[7] *Jeffrey* (1993), 25 C.R. (4th) 104, 84 C.C.C. (3d) 31 (Alta. C.A.).

of the parties to that relationship incompetent to testify for the Crown against the other.[8]

As will be discussed in the section under "Compellability of the Witness" (post), the compellability of a witness must be distinguished from his competence to testify. Although a spouse of an accused may be competent by common law or statute, he or she is not necessarily compellable to give testimony against the accused at the instance of the Crown.

(iv) Children and Mentally Incompetent Persons

Section 16(1) of the *Act* contemplates that there are two persons who may not be competent to give evidence: the first is a person under the age of 14 years; the second is a person who is mentally incompetent. Whenever a person under the age of 14 is called to give evidence, the court is required, before permitting the person to give evidence, to conduct an inquiry to determine

1. whether the person understands the nature of an oath or solemn affirmation; and
2. whether the person is able to communicate the evidence.

Similarly, whenever the testimony of a person is challenged on the basis that he is mentally incompetent, a similar inquiry must take place. Section 16(2) goes on to provide that if the court is satisfied that both conditions are met, then the witness will be entitled to give evidence under oath or by solemn affirmation.

The usual practice is for the judge to question the witness to determine if he or she understands the nature of an oath. The judge's questions must be directed towards determining whether the witness understands the legal consequences of lying under oath and the special obligation to tell the truth in court. As noted earlier, the test is whether "the oath in some way gets a hold on his (the witness) conscience, that there is an appreciation of the significance of testifying in court under oath."[9] Unfortunately the cases offer little assistance to the trial judge on how far he must go to satisfy

---

[8] *Duvivier* (1990), 75 O.R. (2d) 203, 60 C.C.C. (3d) 353 (Gen. Div.), aff'd. on other grounds (1991), 6 C.R.R. (2d) 180, 64 C.C.C. (3d) 20 (Ont. C.A.).

[9] *Supra*, note 2.

the test. This may be because the extent of the inquiry will generally depend upon the age of the child; in other words, an intensive
inquiry will not be necessary when the child is close to 14,[10] as
opposed to a younger child of 8.[11]

However, the fact that a child under the age of 14 or a mentally incompetent person does not understand the nature of an oath
or a solemn affirmation will not necessarily exclude his testimony.
Section 16(3) of the *Act* provides that if the witness is "able to communicate the evidence" and promises to tell the truth, he or she
will be allowed to give unsworn or unaffirmed testimony.[12]

Here the inquiry by the judge must be into the capacity of the
proposed witness to perceive, recollect and communicate, not
whether the witness actually perceives, recollects and communicates
about the events in question.[13] Moreover, as the Supreme Court
stressed in *Marquard*, the test should not be based on any presumption of the incompetency of children to be witnesses; nor is it
intended to make it difficult for children to testify. It merely out-
lines the basic abilities that individuals need to possess if they are
to testify. The phrase "communicate the evidence" in section 16(3)
indicates more than mere verbal ability. The reference to "the evidence" indicates the ability to testify about the matters before the
court. It is necessary to explore in a general way whether the witness is capable of perceiving events, remembering events and com-
municating events to the court. If satisfied that this is the case, the
judge may then receive the child's evidence under section 16(3), after
the witness has promised to tell the truth. It is not necessary to determine in advance that the witness perceived and recollects the very
events at issue in the trial as a condition of ruling that his or her
evidence be received. That is not required of adult witnesses and
should not be required of children.

---

[10] *Fletcher, supra*, note 1.
[11] *L. (J.)* (1990), 54 C.C.C. (3d) 225, 37 O.A.C. 269 (Ont. C.A.).
[12] *D. (R.R.)* (1989), 69 C.R. (3d) 267, 47 C.C.C. (3d) 97 (Sask. C.A.).
[13] *Marquard* (1994), 25 C.R. (4th) 1, 85 C.C.C. (3d) 193 (S.C.C.).

(c) Compellability

(i) The Accused and Co-Accused

To say that a witness is compellable means that the law authorizes either side to call the witness to give evidence. However, the fact that a person may be competent to testify does not necessarily mean that he is automatically compellable to testify. Although the general rule is that all competent witnesses are also compellable, there are a number of exceptions.

The most notable exception is the accused. Although an accused is competent to testify, he is not compellable. However, if he elects to testify, he cannot refuse to answer questions which may incriminate him. He must submit to cross-examination on any issue relating to the case, subject to a limited discretion in the trial judge to prevent cross-examination on a previous criminal record where it might unduly prejudice, mislead or confuse the trier of fact.[14]

A person who is jointly charged and tried with another accused is not compellable to give evidence either by the prosecution or by a co-accused at his own trial. But if his trial is severed from the trial of his co-accused by a judge's order for a separate trial or if he is charged separately by the Crown with the same offence as a co-accused, he becomes an ordinary witness at the trial of the co-accused. Although he may not be compelled to testify at his own trial, he is compellable to testify either for the prosecution or for the defence at the separate trial of his co-accused.

(ii) Spouse of the Accused

When section 4(1) of the *Act* made an accused's spouse a competent witness for the defence, that spouse also became a compellable witness for the defence. However, since a spouse is not competent to testify for the prosecution, he or she is not compellable to testify for the prosecution subject to two exceptions.

The first is the common law exception, preserved by section 4(5) of the *Act,* which allows the prosecution to call the accused's spouse as a witness without the accused's consent where the

---

[14] *Corbett* (1988), 64 C.R. (3d) 1, 41 C.C.C. (3d) 385 (S.C.C.).

common law permitted it. The common law made it an exception where the evidence disclosed that the spouse's person, liberty or health had been threatened by the accused spouse. The second exception is set out in sections 4(2) and (4) of the *Act*. There husbands and wives are compellable against one another with respect to certain offences (generally sexual offences and assaults against children) specified in those sections. The purpose is to ensure that spouses will testify against one another where an offence has been committed against children, particularly their own. Before the enactment of these sections, children who had been physically or sexually assaulted by one parent could not count upon the other parent to testify against the accused.

It is important at this stage to draw a distinction between a "communication" made by husbands and wives to one another and an "observation" by one spouse of the conduct of the other. The two exceptions which allow the prosecution to compel a husband or wife to testify against the other who may be accused of a crime is clearly applicable to observations made by that spouse. However, section 4(3) of the *Act* has created some uncertainty as to whether a husband or wife may be compelled by the prosecution to disclose a marital communication. Section 4(3) provides that,

> 4(3) No husband is compellable to disclose any communication made to him by his wife during their marriage, and no wife is compellable to disclose any communication made to her by her husband during their marriage.

In *St. Jean*[15] Mr. Justice Kaufman said,

> It seems to me that it would not make sense to make a spouse competent and compellable, only to put severe restrictions on the scope of his or her testimony.

However, not all courts have agreed with his observation. Some have concluded that section 4(3) still limits the extent of spousal compulsion to what a spouse observed the other do; a spouse is not compellable by the prosecution to disclose any communication made by his or her spouse during marriage.[16]

---

[15] (1976), 34 C.R.N.S. 378, 32 C.C.C. (2d) 438, (Que. C.A.), at p. 441 (C.C.C.).

[16] *Jean and Piesinger* (1979), 7 C.R. (3d) 338, 46 C.C.C. (3d) 176 (Alta. C.A.); *Re Mailloux* (1980), 30 C.R. (3d) 121, 55 C.C.C. (2d) 193 (Ont. C.A.); *Zylstra* (1994), 88 C.C.C. (3d) 347 (Ont. Gen. Div.).

(d) Refreshing The Witness's Memory

A witness, who is called upon to testify weeks, months or even years after an event, may find that once he steps into the witness box, his memory has failed him on some crucial issues. The rule is that a witness may refresh his memory while in the witness box from any record of the event which he has with him provided, (a) that he made the note of the event himself or, if it was made by another person, he verified the accuracy of the other person's note, and (b) the note was written by him, or the record of another person was verified by him shortly after the event when the facts were fresh in his memory.[17]

Unfortunately, in imposing these conditions, the courts have failed to distinguish between what is known as "past recollection recorded" and "present memory revived." "Past recollection recorded" refers to the situation where the witness has no memory of the events. Here the witness is relying upon his own notes or the notes made by others which he verified at the time they were made. Obviously, then, what is important is the accuracy of witness's notes, not his recollection because he has none. In such instance, counsel will seek to have the notes themselves admitted in evidence as an exhibit for consideration by the judge or jury. But since the opposing side cannot effectively test by cross-examination the accuracy of notes made at an earlier time, the court must first be satisfied that the notes were made in close proximity to the event. In other words, before the court may admit the notes themselves as "past recollection recorded", it must be satisfied that at the time they were made by the witness or by another and verified by the witness, the events were fresh in the witness's mind. Common sense tells us that unless the notes were made when the event was fresh in the witness's mind, there is a serious risk they may contain errors.

"Present memory revived", on the other hand, refers to the situation where the witness has a recollection of the events but wishes to use the notes to jog his memory. The witness does not wish to have the notes admitted as evidence. In such instance, the court need not be as concerned with the proximity in time between the event and when the note was recorded.

---

[17] *Gwozdowski* (1973), 10 C.C.C. (2d) 434 (Ont. C.A.).

Canadian cases, however, have not paid much attention to this distinction.[18] Indeed, they have insisted that in either situation, a witness should not be allowed to use his notes to assist him while giving his evidence unless the notes were made "shortly after the event". What has been considered "shortly after the event" has generally depended upon the circumstances surrounding the event that was recorded. In other words, what the court's have insisted upon is that the notes of the event or the verification of another's record be made when the facts were fresh in the witness' memory.[19]

The reason why Canadian courts have not given much consideration to this distinction is probably because the counsel who calls a witness will not usually ask that witness whether he is relying on his notes or his memory unless he is specifically seeking to have the notes admitted as "past memory recorded." Thus once the witness has read the notes either before trial or during the course of giving his testimony, it may be difficult for the cross-examiner to determine whether the witness is relying on the notes, or his memory of the event, or both.

Is a witness who relies on his notes required to produce them to the opposing counsel for cross-examination? At one time, the rule was that a witness was only required to produce his notes if he relied upon them while testifying in court; if he used the notes to refresh his memory before court, they were not admissible.[20] The irrationality of this distinction is self-evident. All it did was to encourage witnesses to memorize their notes before they came to court.

Today, it is generally accepted that any witness who refreshes his memory from notes or any statement which either he or anyone else has prepared prior to trial or uses those notes to assist him during his testimony must produce them to the opposing counsel for cross-examination.[21] This approach makes more sense. If a witness refreshes his memory before trial or relies upon notes or any document at trial, then what he says when he gives testimony may be essentially the information contained in those notes. Opposing counsel should be allowed to examine the notes to consider whether

---

[18] *B. (A.J.)* (1994), 90 C.C.C. (3d) 210 (Nfld. C.A.).

[19] *Supra*, note 17.

[20] *Kerenko* (1964), 45 C.R. 291, [1965] 3 C.C.C. 52 (Man. C.A.).

[21] *Catling* (1986), 29 C.C.C. (3d) 168 (Alta. C.A.); *Morgan* (1993), 80 C.C.C. (3d) 16 (Ont. C.A.).

they are consistent with the witness's oral testimony. Opposing counsel will also be allowed to have the notes marked as an exhibit if he wishes to show that there is a discrepancy between those notes and the witness's testimony. He may also wish to attack the accuracy of the notes by questioning the timeliness of the record and the possibility of invention.

(e) Adverse Or Hostile Witnesses

(i) Generally

As was pointed out earlier, the side who calls a witness is not allowed to ask that witness leading questions, that is, questions that directly or indirectly suggest the answer to the witness. Occasionally, however, a witness may have a lapse of memory or his testimony may turn out to be inconsistent with what he said in a previous oral or written statement. In the case of a written statement, this situation may be remedied by simply showing the witness his previous statement and asking him to read it over. When this happens, the witness is, in effect, being allowed to refresh his memory.[22]

If the previous inconsistent statement was an oral one, then counsel is entitled to draw his witness's attention to the circumstances surrounding the making of the statement and ask him if he made it. But what happens if the witness cannot remember the previous inconsistent statement, or denies making it, or admits making it but says that it is false? One method of solving this problem is to call other evidence to contradict the witness's testimony. Another is to apply to have the witness declared "hostile." Once a witness is declared hostile, he may be cross-examined, not only with respect to his previous statement, but on the whole of his evidence, or what is commonly called "at large".

The traditional view has been that "a hostile witness is a witness who, from the manner in which he gives his evidence, shows that he is not desirous of telling the truth to the court".[23] In other words, to have your own witness declared "hostile" so that you can cross-examine him, that witness must show some manifest

---

[22] *Coffin* (1956), 23 C.R. 1, 114 C.C.C. 1 (Que. C.A.).
[23] *Coles v. Coles* (1866), L.R. 1 P.70.

hostility or animosity towards you. The judge must determine this by observing his general attitude or demeanour in the witness stand and assessing the substance of his evidence.

Section 9(1) of the *Act* is an attempt to codify the common law. It provides,

> 9(1) A party producing a witness shall not be allowed to impeach his credit by general evidence of bad character, but if the witness, in the opinion of the court, proves adverse, the party may contradict him by other evidence, or, by leave of the court, may prove that the witness made at other times a statement inconsistent with his present testimony, but before the last mentioned proof can be given the circumstances of the supposed statement, sufficient to designate the particular occasion, shall be mentioned to the witness, and he shall be asked whether or not he did make the statement.

This section starts off by stating the general rule that a person calling a witness may not "impeach his credit by general evidence of bad character." Unfortunately, the draftsman of this legislation then went on to misstate the law by requiring the court to first find the witness to be adverse before he could be contradicted by "other evidence". Fortunately, the courts have ignored this condition precedent and have allowed the calling of other evidence to contradict a witness.

Section 24 of the *Ontario Evidence Act*[24] also codifies the common law with respect to civil proceedings. Although, it is cast in similar language, it does not require that there be first a finding of adversity before the witness may be impeached by other evidence. Moreover, in *Wawanesa Mutual Insurance Co. v. Hanes*,[25] the Ontario Court of Appeal held that the word "adverse" should be given its ordinary meaning of "opposed in interest" and not the restricted meaning of "hostile". This means that in determining whether the witness is "adverse", the judge is not limited to a consideration only of his demeanour or attitude in the witness box. The Court also held that the judge could consider a witness's prior inconsistent statement in determining whether he was adverse.

However, not all courts accepted that this interpretation applied to section 9(1) of the *Act*. The result was that in 1969, section 9(2) was added. It provides,

---

[24] R.S.O. 1990, c. E.23.
[25] [1963] 1 C.C.C. 176 (C.A.).

(2) Where the party producing a witness alleges that the witness made at other times a statement in writing, or reduced to writing, inconsistent with his present testimony, the court may, without proof that the witness is adverse, grant leave to that party to cross-examine the witness as to the statement and the court may consider the cross-examination in determining whether in the opinion of the court the witness is adverse.

This section is legislative recognition of the fact that the court is not required to first make a finding of adversity before cross-examination may be permitted by the court on a prior inconsistent statement. However, it must be noted that section 9(2) only applies to "a statement in writing, or reduced to writing". In *Milgaard*[26] the Saskatchewan Court of Appeal proposed the following procedure to be followed where this situation arises,

1. Counsel should advise the court that he desires to make an application under s.9(2) of the Canada Evidence Act.
2. When the court is so advised, the court should direct the jury to retire.
3. Upon retirement of the jury, counsel should advise the trial judge of the particulars of the application and produce for him the alleged statement in writing or the writing to which the statement has been reduced.
4. The trial judge should read the statement, or writing, and determine whether, in fact, there is an inconsistency between the statement or writing and the evidence the witness has given in court. If he decides that there is no inconsistency, then that is the end of the matter. If he finds that there is an inconsistency, he should then call upon counsel to prove the statement or writing.
5. Counsel should then prove the statement or writing. This may be done by producing the statement or writing to the witness. If the witness admits the statement, or the statement reduced to writing, such proof is sufficient. If the witness does not admit it, counsel should then provide the necessary proof by other evidence.
6. If the witness admits making the statement, counsel for the opposing party should have the right to cross-examine as to the circumstances under which the statement was made. A similar right to cross-examine should be granted if the statement is proved by other witnesses. It may be that he will be able to estab-

---

[26] (1971), 14 C.R.N.S. 34, 2 C.C.C. (2d) 206 (Sask. C.A.).

lish that there were circumstances which would render it improper for the trial judge to permit the cross-examination, notwithstanding the apparent inconsistencies. The opposing counsel, too, should have the right to call evidence as to factors relevant to obtaining the statement, for the purpose of attempting to show that cross-examination should not be permitted.
7. The trial judge should then decide whether or not he will permit the cross-examination. If so, the jury should be recalled.

One thing that should be stressed when counsel is proceeding under section 9(2) is that until the witness is declared adverse, cross-examination is limited to the statement that counsel says is a previous inconsistent statement. However, once the court rules that the witness is adverse, he may then be cross-examined at large, that is on his entire evidence.

What steps may counsel take if the previous statement is an oral one? Until the decision of the Ontario Court of Appeal in 1982 in *Cassibo*,[27] the general view was that a judge could not consider a previous inconsistent oral statement in determining whether a witness was adverse because section 9(2) was restricted to previous written statements or ones reduced to writing. The *Cassibo* case rejected the notion that section 9(2) was such a compromise and held that a previous oral statement could be considered under section 9(1) of the *Act*.

Finally, as has already been noted, in deciding whether a person is adverse, the court is not restricted to relying only on the inconsistency in his testimony or the answers that he gives. The court may also determine that a witness is adverse by observing his general attitude or demeanour in the witness stand, by the substance of his evidence and any other contradictory evidence.

(ii) Use That Can be Made of a Prior Inconsistent Statement

What use can be made of a prior inconsistent statement? Until recently, the common law rule has been that if the witness denies making the statement or says that it is false, then no use can be made of it whatsoever. The trier of fact is only entitled to accept the prior inconsistent statement for its truth where the witness adopts

---

[27] (1982), 70 C.C.C. (2d) 498 (Ont. C.A.).

that statement as the truth during his testimony in the witness stand.[28] However, if the witness insists that he did not make the statement or that it is false, the trier is not entitled to accept the prior inconsistent statement as the truth even if he does not believe the witness's testimony. The only use that can be made of that prior inconsistent statement is to cancel out or neutralize the witness's testimony given in court. In other words, it can only be used in assessing the credibility of the testimony given by the witness.

Although a number of reasons have been advanced for the rule, it seems to be generally accepted that it is because what the witness said on a prior occasion is hearsay (which will be discussed in Part B). One concern is that what the witness said on a prior occasion was not said under oath or solemn affirmation. Another is that the judge or jury had no opportunity to observe the witness's demeanour when it was said. Finally, the other side did not have the opportunity to cross-examine the witness when he made the statement.

However, not everyone has agreed with the logic of this rule. Mr. Justice Estey, in a dissenting judgment in *McInroy*[29] could not understand why a witness's prior inconsistent statement could not be considered for its truth as well for the credibility of the witness. Even though the prior inconsistent statement was hearsay, he could not see why the rule should be enforced where the witness was in the witness box and available for cross-examination. Others have argued that the lack of opportunity by the judge and jury to observe the demeanour of the witness at the time that the statement was made, and thus to assess credibility based on that demeanour, is overstated. They point out that the opportunity to observe the witness at trial denying or professing not to remember making the statement can give the judge and jury insight into the truthfulness of the prior statement. Others argue that the power of an oath as a means of ensuring reliability of evidence must be discounted. Moreover, they note that the witness is under oath when he testifies at trial.

All of these various considerations were recently reviewed by Chief Justice Lamer of the Supreme Court of Canada in *K.G.B.*[30] There the Court decided that the time had come for this orthodox rule to be replaced by a new one recognizing the changed means

---

[28] *Deacon* (1947), 3 C.R. 265, 89 C.C.C. 1 (S.C.C.); *Kuldip* (1990), 1 C.R. (4th) 285, 61 C.C.C. (3d) 385 (S.C.C.).

[29] (1979), 5 C.R. (3d) 125, 42 C.C.C. (2d) 481 (S.C.C.).

[30] (1993), 19 C.R. (4th) 1, 79 C.C.C. (3d) 257 (S.C.C.).

and methods of proof in modern society. It was felt that changing the rule was not a matter better left to Parliament since it was a judge-made rule, lent itself to judicial reform and was a natural and incremental progression in the development of the law of hearsay in Canada. Chief Justice Lamer stressed that the focal issue for consideration was the comparative reliability of the prior statement and the testimony offered at trial. He felt that the criterion of reliability would be satisfied when the circumstances in which the prior statement was made provided sufficient guarantees of its trustworthiness with respect to the dangers of the absence of oath and the inability of the trier of fact to assess the declarant's demeanour.

The Court concluded that there would be sufficient guarantees of reliability to allow the jury to make substantive use of the statement,

1. if the statement was made under oath, solemn affirmation or solemn declaration following an explicit warning to the witness as to the existence of severe criminal sanctions for the making of a false statement;
2. if the statement was videotaped in its entirety; and
3. if the opposing party, whether the Crown or the defence, had a full opportunity to cross-examine the witness at trial respecting the statement.

The Court, however, did not restrict the admissibility of a prior inconsistent statement for its truth to the satisfaction of these three conditions. It left it open to the trial judge to consider other guarantees of reliability provided that he was satisfied that the circumstances provided adequate assurances of reliability in place of those which the hearsay rule traditionally required.

Chief Justice Lamer summarized the role of the trial judge such that,

> ...in the part of the *voir dire* addressing the new rule, the trial judge must first satisfy him or herself that the indicia of reliability necessary to admit hearsay evidence of prior statements — a warning, oath, solemn affirmation, or solemn declaration, and videotape record, or sufficient substitutes — are present and genuine. If they are, he or she must then examine the circumstances under which the statement was obtained, to satisfy him or herself that the statement supported by the indicia of reliability was made voluntarily if to a person in authority, and that there are no other factors which would tend to bring the administration of justice into disrepute if the statement was admitted as substantive evidence. In most cases, as in this

case, the party seeking to admit the prior inconsistent statements as substantive evidence will have to establish that these requirements have been satisfied on the balance of probabilities. The trial judge is not to decide whether the prior inconsistent statement is true, or more reliable than the present testimony, as that is a matter for the trier of fact. Once this process is complete, and all of its constituent elements satisfied, the trial judge need not issue the standard limiting instruction to the jury, but may instead tell the jury that they may take the statement as substantive evidence of its contents, or, if he or she is sitting alone, make substantive use of the statement, giving the evidence the appropriate weight after taking into account all of the circumstances. In either case, the judge must direct the trier of fact to consider carefully these circumstances in assessing the credibility of the prior inconsistent statement relative to the witness' testimony at trial. For example, where appropriate the trial judge might make specific reference to the significance of the demeanour of the witness at all relevant times (which could include when making the statement, when recanting at trial, and/or when presenting conflicting testimony at trial), the reasons offered by the witness for his or her recantation, any motivation and/or opportunity the witness had to fabricate his or her evidence when making the previous statement or when testifying at trial, the events leading up to the making of the first statement and the nature of the interview at which the statement was made (including the use of leading question, and the existence of pre-statement interview or coaching), corroboration of the facts in the statement by other evidence, and the extent to which the nature of the witness' recantation limits the effectiveness of cross-examination on the previous statement. There may be other factors the trier of fact should consider, and the trial judge should impress upon the trier of fact the importance of carefully assessing all such matters in determining the weight to be afforded prior inconsistent statements as substantive evidence.

Where the prior statement does not have the necessary circumstantial guarantees of reliability, and so cannot pass the threshold test on the *voir dire*, but the party tendering the prior statement otherwise satisfied the requirements of ss. 9(1) or (2) of the *Canada Evidence Act*, the statement may still be tendered into evidence, but the trial judge must instruct the jury in the terms of the orthodox rule.[31]

(f) Protection or Privilege from Answering Questions

When a witness enters the witness box, he is required to answer all questions that are relevant to the facts in issue. The common law, however, has recognized that for reasons of public policy, certain persons should be protected from answering questions touching on certain matters. It does not mean that the questions asked

---

[31] *Ibid.*, pp. 44-45 (C.R.).

by examining counsel nor the answers he seeks are not relevant to the issues in the case. They may be very relevant. It simply means that the courts have concluded that society, as a whole, would be better served if some witnesses were protected from revealing certain information even though that information was important and crucial to the determination of the case.

What kind of information is protected?

(i) The Privilege Against Self-Incrimination.

At one time, anyone accused of heresy or some other crime could be brought before a judge or some other public official and ordered to take an oath to answer truthfully all the questions that might be put to him. He was not told of the specific crime that he was suspected to have committed nor the names of the witnesses against him. If he refused to take the oath or answer the questions put to him, he was thrown into prison and kept there until he agreed to answer the questions.

By the beginning of the seventeenth century, many persons summoned for questioning refused to take the oath and claimed that "no man should be required to incriminate himself." The prosecution of John Lilburne brought the matter to the attention of the courts and Parliament and, by the end of the seventeenth century, the claim of privilege became firmly established in all courts. It was enshrined in the *American Bill of Rights* as the Fifth Amendment on September 25th, 1789. In Canada, it was given constitutional recognition by section 11(c) of the *Charter of Rights and Freedoms*[32] in 1982. Section 11(c) provides that,

> Any person charged with an offence has the right
>
> > (c) not to be compelled to be a witness in proceedings against that person in respect of the offence.

Section 11(c) thus protects an accused from being forced to enter the witness box to give evidence. However, if he voluntarily chooses to testify, then he loses his privilege of silence and is treated like any other witness. Once an accused chooses to testify, section

---

[32] *The Canadian Charter of Rights and Freedoms*, Part 1 of the Constitution Act, 1982, being schedule B to the Canada Act 1982 (U.K.), 1982, c. 11.

5(1) of the *Act* requires him to answer all questions that are put to him by counsel or the judge, and any testimony that he gives may be considered by the judge and jury in determining his guilt or innocence on the charge. However, section 5(2) of the *Act* guarantees the accused (or any witness who testifies) that in exchange for being compelled to answer a question put to him, his testimony at trial is protected from being used against him in any other criminal proceeding against him except a later prosecution for perjury in the giving of that evidence. Similar protection is guaranteed under provincial evidence statutes. Such protection is also given constitutional recognition by section 13 of the *Charter*.

Section 13 provides,

> A witness who testified in any proceedings has the right not to have any incriminating evidence so given used to incriminate that witness in any other proceedings, except in a prosecution for perjury or for the giving of contradictory evidence.

The difference between section 5(2) of the *Act* and section 13 is that section 5(2) requires the witness at the first proceeding to object to answering the question to trigger the protection granted by that section. Section 13 of the *Charter* automatically gives the witness protection. Moreover, section 5(2) only protects the witness from a prosecution for perjury. Section 13 also protects the witness from a prosecution for giving contradictory evidence contrary to section 136 of the *Criminal Code*.[33]

Although the testimony of an accused or any witness may not be used to incriminate him at a later proceeding, his evidence may be used to test or impeach his credibility at that later proceeding. For example, it is open for an accused or a witness to be asked questions about the apparent inconsistencies between the testimony given at the previous proceedings and the testimony that he is now giving so long as the questions are not questions incriminating him.[34]

(ii) Spousal Privilege

As noted earlier, an accused's spouse is not competent nor compellable as a witness for the prosecution unless the offence charged

---

[33] R.S.C. 1985, c. C-46.
[34] *Kuldip, supra*, note 28.

is one of those listed in subsections (2) and (4) of section 4 of the *Act* or is subject to the common law exception preserved by section 4(5). The common law exception arises in those cases where the charge affects the person, health or liberty of the spouse of the accused. For a long time, there was some uncertainty in Canada as to whether the charge itself had to specifically allege a threat to the spouse or if it was enough that the evidence itself disclosed such a threat. In *D.P.P. v. Blady*,[35] the English Court of Criminal Appeal had decided that the nature of the charge must affect a spouse's health or liberty. However, Canadian cases eventually began to adopt a liberal approach allowing a spouse to testify simply where the evidence reveals that his or her health or liberty is affected.[36]

Although the common law exception extends to cases involving the health or liberty of a spouse, it does not, ironically, apply where the health or liberty of a child of the accused is involved. In other words, at common law, a wife was able to testify against her husband where he beat her up but not where he beat up their child. An attempt to rectify this situation was made in 1903 by an amendment to the *Act*. That amendment listed a number of offences, primarily sexual offences, where a spouse was both competent and compellable for the prosecution but it omitted simple assaults. In 1983, that omission was corrected by a further amendment to section 4(4).

Of course, spousal privilege against compellability by the prosecution extends only as long as the parties are married at the time of trial and are living together. If the parties are married at the time of the offence but are divorced at the time of trial, then the privilege does not apply.[37] Since the modern justification for the rule is that it promotes marital harmony, it is against common sense that spousal privilege should continue after divorce.

That view has recently supported the argument that spousal privilege should not continue if the parties are separated and there is no reasonable possibility of reconciliation.[38] Nor should spousal incompetence or non-compellability be extended to so-called

---

[35] [1912] 2 K.B. 89.
[36] *Sillars* (1978), 12 C.R. (3d) 202, 45 C.C.C. (2d) 283 (B.C. C.A.) and *Czipps* (1979), 12 C.R. (3d) 193, 48 C.C.C. (2d) 166 (Ont. C.A.).
[37] *Marchand* (1980), 55 C.C.C. (2d) 77 (N.S. C.A.); *Bailey* (1983), 32 C.R. (3d) 337, 4 C.C.C. (3d) 21 (Ont. C.A.).
[38] *Salituro* (1990), 78 C.R. (3d) 68, 56 C.C.C. (3d) 350 (Ont. C.A.), approved S.C.C. (1992), 9 C.R. (4th) 324.

"common law marriages" or similar relationships since they are not recognized by law on other grounds.[39]

In *Salituro*,[40] Mr. Justice Iacobucci wrote,

> Absent parliamentary intervention, I would conclude that changing the common law rule to make spouses who are irreconcilably separated competent witnesses for the prosecution would be appropriate. Although the principles upon which this change is based would appear to favour abolishing the rule entirely and making all spouses competent witnesses under all circumstances, policy considerations and uncertainty as to the consequences of such change suggest that a more cautious approach is appropriate. The parties before us did not argue for such a change, and in my opinion a far reaching change of this kind is best left to the legislature. However, expanding the exceptions to the common law rule to include irreconcilably separated spouses is precisely the kind of incremental change which the courts can and should make. The courts are custodians of the common law, and it is their duty to see that the common law reflects the emerging need and value of our society.

As noted previously, a distinction must be drawn between a "communication" made by husbands and wives to one another and an "observation" by one spouse of the conduct of the other. Section 4(3) of the *Act* provides that no spouse is compellable "to disclose any communication made 'to him or her by the other spouse' during their marriage". The prevailing view seems to be that all marital communications continue to be protected by section 4(3) of the *Act*,[41] although the issue is not entirely free from doubt.[42] What is clear, however, is that any protected marital communication must be testimonial in nature. Spousal privilege will not prevent the admission into evidence of a document written by the accused and sent to his wife which is found during a search of the accused's house.[43] Moreover, the privilege is limited to the spouses themselves. Third persons who overhear, either intentionally or accidentally, a marital communication are compellable by the prosecution to testify about what they overheard.[44]

---

[39] *Duvivier* (1990), 60 C.C.C. (3d) 353 (Ont. Gen. Div.), aff'd 64 C.C.C. (3d) 20 (Ont. C.A.).

[40] *Supra*, note 38.

[41] *Jean and Piesinger* (1979), 7 C.R. (3d) 338, 46 C.C.C. (3d) 176 (Alta. C.A.); *Re Mailloux* (1980), 30 C.R. (3d) 121, 55 C.C.C. (2d) 193 (Ont. C.A.); *Zylstra* (1994), 88 C.C.C. (3d) 347 (Ont. Gen. Div.).

[42] *St. Jean* (1976), 34 C.R.N.S. 378, 32 C.C.C. (2d) 438 (Que. C.A.).

[43] *Kotapski* (1981), 66 C.C.C. (2d) 78 (Que.S.C.), aff'd 13 C.C.C. (3d) 185 (C.A.) leave to appeal to S.C.C. refused (1984), 57 N.R. 318 (S.C.C.).

[44] *Rumping v. D.P.P.*, [1964] A.C. 814 (H.L.).

What does not appear to have ever been dealt with in any reported Canadian decision is whether a communication made by one spouse to the other before marriage is protected by section 4(3). The section clearly speaks of "any communication made...during their marriage" and would thereby exclude communications made before marriage. On the other hand, it is arguable that if the purpose of the section is to promote marital harmony, then it should be interpreted to include all communications made prior to or during marriage provided that the marriage is bona fide and subsisting at the time of the trial of the accused spouse.

(iii) Solicitor/client Privilege

What a person says to his lawyer in the latter's professional capacity and intended to be confidential is privileged. Neither the lawyer nor the client can be compelled to disclose the contents of that information.[45] The basis of the rule is this: it is thought to be in the best interests of society as a whole that a person be allowed to consult with his legal adviser openly and freely knowing that what he tells his legal adviser cannot be revealed. There is, however, one exception to this rule. It is not in the public interest that a person be allowed to consult with a lawyer to obtain advice on how to commit a crime.[46] Such a communication is outside the scope of the rule and is not protected from being revealed by the solicitor.

It should be pointed out that the communication does not have to be given directly to the lawyer; it may be given to the lawyer's assistant or anyone acting under the lawyer's supervision. Moreover, even if a person changes lawyers, the information that he gave to his previous lawyer is still protected from disclosure. The protection also extends to information given by two or more persons to their lawyer in connection with the same matter.

It is important to stress that the privilege extends only to a communication made by the client to his solicitor. It does not extend to any real evidence that a client may have given to his solicitor for safe keeping. For example, if a client leaves with his solicitor evidence of a crime, such as a weapon or bloody shirt, no privilege attaches to these items. Indeed, the solicitor may be compelled to

---

[45] *Bencardino* (1973), 24 C.R.N.S. 173, 15 C.C.C. (2d) 342 (Ont. C.A.).
[46] *Cox and Railton* (1884), 14 Q.B.D. 153.

testify for the prosecution that he received these items from his client.

The client, but not the lawyer, may waive a solicitor-client privilege. However, if he waives part of it, then he cannot claim protection for the balance of the communication. If he waives any part of the privilege, he loses protection for the entire communication.[47]

(iv) Identity Of Informers

Law enforcement officers often depend upon professional informers to furnish them with information about criminal activities. The law therefore recognizes that it is in the best interests of society as a whole that people with important information about the commission of a crime be encouraged to come forward and give that information to the police without fear of disclosure. The law thus protects a witness for the Crown from answering questions that would have the effect of disclosing the identity of the informer.[48]

This protection is, however, not absolute. If the court is persuaded that the identity of the informant would be material to demonstrate the innocence of the accused, then the court may order the witness to disclose the informant's identity.[49] For example, section 7 of the *Charter* ensures that everyone has the right "to life, liberty and security of the person and the right not to be deprived thereof except in accordance with the principles of fundamental justice." The principles of fundamental justice entitle everyone accused of a crime to make "full answer and defence". An example of where this occurred was the case of *Hunter*.[50] In that case, the defence were seeking to attack a search warrant that had been used to search the accused's residence where narcotics were discovered. It was held that, in the circumstances of that case, disclosure of the identity of the informer was crucial to the defence. The Crown was given the option of either disclosing the informant's identity, proceeding on a warrantless search or withdrawing the prosecution.

Another exception which allows the court to order disclosure is where the informer has acted as an agent provocateur. Disclosure may also be ordered where the accused seeks to establish that a

---

[47] *Supra*, note 43.
[48] *Hunter* (1987), 57 C.R. (3d) 1, 34 C.C.C. (3d) 14 (Ont. C.A.).
[49] *Bisaillon v. Keable* (1983), 37 C.R. (3d) 289, 7 C.C.C. (3d) 385 (S.C.C.).
[50] *Supra*, note 48.

search and seizure of his premises was not undertaken on reasonable grounds and therefore contravened section 8 of the *Charter*.[51]

(v) Public Interest Privilege

The law recognizes that it is not in the public interest to disclose certain information regarding governmental activities. At the same time, it also recognizes that for the administration of justice to operate properly, all litigants should have access to all evidence that may be of assistance to the fair disposition of issues arising in litigation. What the court must try to do is balance these two competing interests. It will depend, as one judge has said, on "changing social conditions and the role of government in society at various times".[52]

(vi) Other Privileges

The common law recognizes two other instances where persons may be protected from disclosing information. The first involves deliberations carried out by jurors in the jury room. No juror may be required to divulge what was said by any juror during deliberations except for the purposes of an investigation of a charge of obstructing justice involving a fellow juror. Not only is a juror protected from being compelled to disclose that information, he is guilty of contempt of court if he does. Moreover, section 649 of the *Code* now makes it an offence for a juror to disclose such information.

There a several reasons for the rule. One reason is that verdicts are intended to be final and jurors should not be required to explain why they reached a particular verdict. If a juror was required to disclose what took place, it would encourage dissatisfied litigants from using every means to find out what went on in the jury room in an effort to show that the result was not according to law and this would be contrary to public policy.[53] Another is to encourage jurors, while deliberating their verdict, to engage in frank discus-

---

[51] *Scott* (1990), 2 C.R. (4th) 153, 61 C.C.C. (3d) 300 (S.C.C.).
[52] *Carey* (1986) 30 C.C.C. (3d) 498 (S.C.C.), per LaForest J. at p. 506.
[53] *Perras* (No. 2) (1974), 18 C.C.C. (2d) 47 (Sask. C.A.).

sion without fear that what they say may be publicly disclosed by another juror. Finally, the recent attention by the media to high profile cases gives added importance to the rule. It ensures that jurors are protected from harassment by investigative reporters and prevents jurors from financially exploiting their duties by selling accounts of the jury's deliberations to the media.

Finally, diplomats are protected from disclosure of information. This common law rule is based upon the theory that although the courts generally have jurisdiction over foreign subjects who are present in Canada, they should respect representatives of the government of another country. Such immunity, however, is not absolute where the safety of the country is imperiled.[54]

(vii) No Privilege

There is a misconception by the public generally that persons such as doctors, psychiatrists, priests and journalists have the right to refuse to divulge information given to them by patients, penitents and informants. No such common law privilege exists. The reason is that the courts have considered that the public interest in the search for truth far outweighs the protection of confidentiality in such cases.[55]

Similarly, the privilege contained in section 10(5) of the *Divorce Act*[56] which precludes the admissibility of "anything said or of any admission or communication made in the course of assisting spouses to achieve a reconciliation" only applies where the statements for which the claim is made is "in a divorce proceeding" and to a "person nominated by a court under this section to assist spouses to achieve a reconciliation".[57] Although the common law recognizes a privilege in matrimonial disputes for the purpose of promoting spouses to reconcile, there is no such common law privilege recognized by the criminal law outside of the plea bargaining structure.

Nevertheless, some judges, particularly in civil cases, have been loath to compel such witnesses to disclose information given in con-

---

[54] *Rose* (1946), 3 C.R. 277, 88 C.C.C. 114 (Que. C.A.).
[55] *S. (R.J.)* (1985), 45 C.R. (3d) 161, 19 C.C.C. (3d) 115 (Ont. C.A.).
[56] R.S.C. 1985, Chap. 3 (2nd Supp.).
[57] *Pabani* (1994), 29 C.R. (4th) 364, 17 O.R. (3d) 659 (Ont. C.A.).

fidence to them;[58] other judges have ordered the information to be disclosed but have refused to impose any penalty, or have imposed a nominal one, for the refusal to do so. By doing so, the judge has not recognized a legal privilege. He or she has simply refused to impose sanctions on the witness for refusing to divulge the confidential information.

A recent decision of the Supreme Court of Canada, however, has recognized that there may be case-by-case instances where a judge may allow a person to withhold disclosure of a confidential communication. In *Fosty*,[59] the Court recognized that there are two types of privilege: the first is "blanket privilege" (or what is also known as prima facie, common-law or class privilege); the other is "case-by-case privilege". Blanket privilege is the kind of privilege that has been discussed previously. However, if an accused can show that the relationship between himself and his confessor satisfies certain pre-conditions, the courts will generally rule that the confession was privileged.

The pre-conditions used are based on the test set out by the late Professor Wigmore in his text "Evidence in Trial at Common Law".[60] The test was this:

1. The communication must originate in a confidence that it will not be disclosed;
2. The element of confidentiality must be essential to the full and satisfactory maintenance of the relationship between the parties;
3. The relationship must be one which in the opinion of the community ought to be sedulously fostered;
4. The injury that would inure to the relationship by the disclosure of the communication would be greater than the benefit gained for the correct disposal of the litigation.

3. DOCUMENTARY EVIDENCE

(a) Generally

Direct or circumstantial evidence of a fact in issue may also be proved by a document. In order to prove the authenticity of a

---

[58] *Dembie v. Dembie* (1963), 21 R.F.L. 46 (Ont. H.C.).
[59] (1991), 8 C.R. (4th) 368 (*sub nom. R. v. Gruenke*), 67 C.C.C. (3d) 289 (S.C.C.).
[60] *McNaughton*, rev. ed. (1961), vol. 8, para. 2285.

document, it is usually necessary to call as a witness the person who made it so that he can identify it. However, proof as to authorship can also be established by circumstantial evidence such as the finding of the document in the possession of someone, an admission of ownership or authorship, or proof by a handwriting expert.[61] In such instance, it is still necessary for a witness to be asked to identify the document and to give evidence that will tend to connect it with a fact in issue.

Let us assume for example that the accused is charged with forging a cheque. If someone is able to testify that he saw the accused writing out the cheque and can identify the particular document, that is direct evidence from which a judge or jury can conclude that the accused committed the crime. Let us assume, on the other hand, that no one saw him write the cheque but a witness is familiar with his handwriting. If the witness is able to identify the writing and signature on the cheque as belonging to the accused, that will not be direct evidence that the accused forged the cheque, but will be circumstantial evidence from which a judge or jury can draw that inference.

Quite often, however, a document may be found in the possession of the accused that is incriminating in nature but no one is able to say that they saw the accused prepare it and no one can identify his signature. Let us assume, for example, that the accused, a butcher, is charged with selling horse meat which he fraudulently represented as beef. Assume that the police execute a search warrant at his home and find invoices from a horse rancher in Texas which indicate that certain horses were sold to the accused on a certain date. It is obvious that these invoices are relevant to the issue of whether the accused has been buying horses and selling them as beef. On the other hand, there is also the possibility that the documents are not relevant to the prosecution at all and simply indicate that the accused purchased some horses that he may still own or that he may have sold intact to someone else. It is also possible that the documents were fabricated by someone who wishes to harm the accused. Nevertheless, the courts have held that all documents found in the possession of an accused, which are relevant to an issue before the court, are admissible as evidence of knowledge of their contents and may be considered by the judge and jury on the issue of

---

[61] *Bloomfield* (1973), 21 C.R.N.S. 97 (N.B. C.A.).

his guilt. The prosecution is not required to first prove, as a condition of admissibility, that the accused has knowledge of the contents of the document.[62] The weight to be attached to those documents will depend upon all of the circumstances of the case.

(b) Best Evidence Rule

The Best Evidence rule is a rule of evidence that requires the side that relies upon a document to produce the original of it unless the original was destroyed or cannot be found, or it is impossible or impractical to produce. For example, it may be impossible or impractical to produce the original if it is in the possession of someone in another country and a Canadian court has no jurisdiction to order its production.

The rule dates back to the very early common law when witnesses did not testify before juries and was connected with the doctrine of "profert" in pleading, which required a party relying upon a document as a ground of action or defence to produce it bodily to the court. As the law developed and witnesses were allowed to testify, the rule was justified on the basis that it prevented fraud. It was presumed that if the original document existed, then it was likely being withheld for some sinister motive. As well, there was a concern that a copy of a document, made by hand in those days, might be inaccurate.

Today with modern photostatting machines, it is often possible to produce a document that cannot be distinguished from the original and the best evidence rule is often relaxed. On the other hand, the same technology allows production of an authentic-looking "copy" that may actually be a forgery made up of several documents pasted together. Nevertheless, lawyers will frequently admit that a particular document is a photocopy of the original and that it will not be necessary to comply with the Best Evidence rule. However, if the opposing side is not prepared to agree with the production of a photostat or a copy, then the witness through whom the document is introduced must give some explanation as to why the original cannot be produced and, at least, be able to say that the copy is an exact reproduction of the original. In such instance, the court will generally admit it and the issue as to whether it is

---

[62] *Turlon* (1989), 70 C.R. (3d) 376, 49 C.C.C. (3d) 186 (Ont. C.A.).

an exact copy of the original will go to the question of the weight of the evidence but not its admissibility.

4. ARTICLES AND THINGS

Another form of evidence, in addition to oral and documentary evidence, may be an article or thing that is connected with the crime such as a gun or a knife, or in the case of a stolen article, the thing itself. This is known as real evidence because it can be seen, touched, heard or tested by the judge and jury. Where such evidence is being tendered, it is generally necessary for a witness to identify it and explain why it is being produced. It will then be made an exhibit (just as a document will be made an exhibit) so that if the verdict is appealed, the Court of Appeal will be able to determine what went on at the trial.

There may be circumstances where it may be impossible or inconvenient to produce the original article. For example, it would hardly add to the decorum of a trial to produce a stolen cow for inspection by the judge and jury, nor would it be practical to produce a stolen automobile. The usual practice is for a photograph to be taken of the particular article and to introduce the photograph in its place. Unless the other side agrees that the photograph is an exact replica of the article, then here again a witness must be called to testify that he took the photograph of the article or that he is familiar with it, and the photograph is an accurate photograph of it.

5. DEMONSTRATIVE EVIDENCE

Visual aids such as photographs, maps, diagrams or flow charts will often be admitted by the judge to assist the judge and jury in reaching their verdict. Whether the photograph, diagram, map, flow chart or any other item will assist the judge and jury, will often depend on the facts of the particular case. A judge may also permit an experiment or demonstration in the courtroom. For example, in *Brooks*,[63] where the defence attacked the testimony of a police officer who said that he took a statement from the accused in eight minutes, the trial judge permitted defence counsel to conduct an

---

[63] (1993), 81 C.C.C. (3d) 428 (Ont. Gen. Div.).

experiment and have the officer duplicate as far as possible the taking of the statement.

Sometimes opposing counsel will object to the introduction of a diagram or a map because it is not drawn to scale or a photograph because it is misleading. In each case, the question of admissibility will depend upon whether the judge feels that the document will assist him and the jury in better understanding the evidence. If it is so distorted that it gives a wrong or a misleading impression, then he will undoubtedly refuse to admit it.[64]

The most difficult question arises in the case of photographs. The first thing that must be established by the side that wishes to introduce a photograph is that it is an accurate depiction of the scene or the subject of the photograph and that it is being offered to assist the trier in determining the issue before him. Often the main objection will be that the photograph, particularly of a victim, may inflame the jury and divert them from their main task or cause them to be prejudiced against the accused. For a long time, the main concern of the court was one of admissibility. Mr. Justice Masten pointed out almost sixty years ago in *O'Donnell*,[65]

> The only question to be considered is were they admissible under the rules of evidence. If they are the effect which they may have on the jury cannot interfere with their admission.

However, with the development of judicial discretion has arisen the recognition that the trial judge has the right to exclude photographs if they are of minor assistance and their prejudicial effect far outweighs that assistance. On the other hand, the corollary of this is that if the photograph will assist the judge and jury in understanding the evidence, it will generally be admitted even it is inflammatory.[66] In each case, the judge must use his discretion to ensure that the accused receives a fair trial.[67]

---

[64] *Valley* (1986), 26 C.C.C. (3d) 207 (Ont. C.A.), leave to appeal to S.C.C. refused (1986), 26 C.C.C. (3d) 207n (S.C.C.).

[65] (1936), 65 C.C.C. 299 (Ont. C.A.), at p. 383.

[66] *Davis* (No. 2) (1977), 35 C.C.C. (2d) 464 (Alta. C.A.).

[67] *Kendall* (1988), 57 C.R. (3d) 249, 35 C.C.C. (3d) 105 (Ont. C.A.); *Wade* (1994), 29 C.R. (4th) 327, 89 C.C.C. (3d) 39 (Ont. C.A.).

PART B

Excluded Evidence

3

Hearsay

1. THE RULE

Probably no rule of evidence is more misunderstood than the rule against hearsay. It is misunderstood because it is commonly believed that it means that a witness may not testify as to what he was told by someone else. Because this is only a partial explanation of the rule, it is important then to start at the beginning.

The first question that must be asked whenever the possibility of hearsay arises is "what is the side calling the witness seeking to prove". For example, let us assume the accused is charged with robbing a bank at 5 minutes after 12:00 o'clock noon and X saw the accused enter the bank at 12:00 o'clock noon. Such evidence is offered, not as direct evidence that the accused robbed the bank, but rather as circumstantial evidence from which a jury can infer that he was in the bank at the time of the robbery. Together with other evidence, it may establish that he was the robber. The rule is that only X may be called to testify that he saw the accused enter the bank at 12:00 noon.

Let us assume, however, that X is unavailable to testify but told Y that he saw the accused enter the bank at 12:00 noon. If the Crown seeks to introduce what X saw through the testimony of Y, that would be hearsay. Y will not be permitted to testify as to what X told him to prove that the accused entered the bank at 12:00 noon.

Why do we prohibit hearsay evidence? Clearly, the fact that X saw the accused enter the bank at 12:00 noon is logically probative of one of the three issues that the Crown must prove. Yet the rules of evidence do not permit Y to tell the court what X told him. Why? The answer is simply this. How can anyone cross-examine Y about what X told him? All Y can do is go on repeating what X told him. There is no way of testing whether X was telling the truth when he told Y that he saw the accused going into the bank at 12:00 noon. Unless X is compelled to come to court where his demeanour can be observed and his evidence tested by cross-examination, there is no way of ensuring that his story is true. Moreover, everyone knows that whenever information is passed from one person to the next, there is a risk that it may be misunderstood. Our system of justice recognizes that someone's life or liberty should not depend upon second-hand information.

Let us assume, however, that X also told Z that he saw the accused enter the bank at 2:00 p.m. and the defence wishes to call Z to say exactly what X told him. Is it hearsay? That will depend upon what the evidence is attempting to prove. Assume that the defence wishes to call the evidence to show that X should not be believed about having seen the accused enter the bank at 12:00 noon because he told Z that he saw him enter the bank at 2:00 p.m. Here it is not being offered to prove that the accused entered the bank at 2:00 p.m., but to show that X was mistaken when he testified that the accused entered the bank at 12:00 noon. In such instance it is admissible. It does not offend the hearsay rule. It is original or first-hand evidence because it is being offered only to prove that X said it happened at 2.00 p.m., that is, just the fact that it was said, not the fact that it is true.

What the law of evidence seeks to ensure is that only original or first-hand evidence will be admitted to prove a fact in issue. Second-hand evidence will not suffice. On the other hand, where the fact in issue is whether a statement was made by someone else, then the statement will be admitted because it bears directly on the issue to be proved. It is still original or first-hand evidence, not second-hand evidence.

2. WHEN IS HEARSAY ALLOWED?

Most legal historians believe that the hearsay rule, like all exclusionary rules, owes its origin to the jury system. The jury was allowed to hear only evidence that was given under oath and subject to cross-examination. Some scholars argue that these two reasons have little substance today. For example, a witness who feels that his moral conscience cannot be bound by the oath is permitted to testify by affirmation. Moreover, juries today are sophisticated enough to know that the mere fact that a person takes an oath does not ensure the truth of his testimony. If anything does promote truth, it is the fear of a prosecution for perjury.

The real reason, today, why hearsay is still excluded is because it cannot be tested by cross-examination. The law requires the person who has first-hand knowledge of the facts to come forward and to testify so that his evidence can be subjected to the scrutiny of cross-examination.

But what if that person is dead or otherwise unavailable to testify? Should the law, confronted with a choice of either accepting second hand evidence or no evidence at all, choose the latter? No sooner was the exclusionary rule of hearsay invented in the late seventeenth century than judges began to realize that unless certain types of hearsay were admitted, serious crimes might go unpunished or litigants denied justice. The result was that the courts began to create certain exceptions to the strict application of the hearsay rule where the declarant was dead.

The rationale underlying these exception was explained by Professor Wigmore this way:

> The purpose and reason of the Hearsay rule is the key to the exceptions to it. The theory of the Hearsay rule is that many possible sources of inaccuracy and untrustworthiness which may lie underneath the bare untested assertion of a witness can best be brought to light and exposed, if they exist, by the test of cross-examination. But this test or security may in a given instance be superfluous; it may be sufficiently clear, in that instance, that the statement offered is free enough from the risk of inaccuracy and untrustworthi-

ness, so that the test of cross-examination would be a work of supererogation. Moreover, the test may be impossible of employment — for example, by reason of the death of the declarant — so that, if his testimony is to be used at all, there is a necessity for taking it in the untested shape.[1]

For almost three centuries, these judicial exceptions to the hearsay rule were strictly applied by the courts. However, in 1970 the Supreme Court of Canada delivered its landmark decision in *Ares v. Venner*.[2] There the court permitted a plaintiff to introduce hospital records of his treatment for a broken leg as declarations made in the ordinary course of duty and as *"prima facie* proof of the facts stated therein" even though the nurses who had made the records were alive and were, in fact, waiting outside the courtroom to testify. Unfortunately, *Ares v. Venner* lay dormant for another twenty years until another landmark decision of the Supreme Court of Canada, *Khan*.[3] This time the court decided to strike out in a new direction. Instead of extending the old exceptions created centuries earlier, the court adopted a new test — "necessity and reliability". The *Khan* decision and the developments it has spawned will be discussed later in this chapter under the heading, "Recent Developments".

3. EXCEPTIONS TO THE HEARSAY RULE

(a) Assertions of Deceased Persons

(i) Dying declarations

Should a victim of a homicide be allowed to identify his killer before he died? A strict application of the hearsay rule would say "no" because his identification evidence would have to be given second-hand by the person who overheard him. However, if such evidence was not admitted, a murderer might be able to escape punishment for his crime. On the other hand, there is always the danger that a person who is dying might try to settle a score with

---

[1] John H. Wigmore, Wigmore on Evidence (3rd ed.), Vol. 5, (Boston: Little, Brown and Co., 1974), para. 1420, p. 202.

[2] (1970), 12 C.R.N.S. 349 (S.C.C.).

[3] (1990), 79 C.R. (3d) 1, 59 C.C.C. (3d) 92 (S.C.C.).

an enemy by falsely accusing him of murder. Faced with these two policy considerations, the courts decided to opt in favour of admitting the evidence for what it was worth. It was argued that anyone going to his maker was unlikely to perjure his soul by dying with a lie on his lips. At the same time, the courts were anxious to ensure that there would be no danger of mistake or an attempt to settle old scores.[4] They did this by creating two conditions that must be satisfied before such evidence would be admitted.

The first was that it could only be allowed in a trial for the murder or manslaughter of the victim who made the declaration. This rule was so strictly applied that in one case, the court refused to accept the dying declaration of a woman on the trial of the person charged with procuring her abortion even though it resulted in her death. The other condition was that the victim must have had a settled hopeless expectation of impending death at the time that he made the declaration. It was believed that a victim's apprehension of death when he made the declaration would ensure its trustworthiness. In other words, a person is unlikely to tell a deliberate lie when he knows that he is dying and has no hope of recovery.

Unfortunately, this latter condition restricts the admissibility of a dying declaration because it cannot always be assumed that a person who is dying knows that he is dying. Moreover, it is unlikely that even the most seriously injured person can appreciate that his life is in danger or that he will be told this by anyone who comes to his aid. Indeed, it is more likely that he will be encouraged to "hang on" until help comes.

Nevertheless, these conditions have been and continue to be strictly applied by the courts.[5] A famous example is the *Bedingfield* case.[6] Bedingfield was charged with the murder of a woman by cutting her throat. At his trial, a prosecution witness testified that she saw the victim running out of the house in which she had just been with Bedingfield. Her throat was almost completely severed. Just before the victim died, she said "Look what Bedingfield has done to me." However, Chief Justice Cockburn refused to permit the witness to repeat what she heard the victim say. The fact that the wound itself was very serious was not enough for the

4 *Schwartzenhauer* (1935), 64 C.C.C. 1 (S.C.C.).
5 *Kharsekin* (1992), 74 C.C.C. (3d) 163 (Nfld. S.C.), reversed on other grounds (1994), 88 C.C.C. (3d) 193 (Nfld. C.A.).
6 (1879), 14 Cox 341.

court to draw the inference that the victim knew that she was dying. Fortunately, Bedingfield was convicted on other evidence.

Recently, in *Kharsekin*,[7] the victim of a knife attack told a physician who was attending him that he had been wounded by the accused. An hour later, he again identified the accused as his attacker in response to an inquiry. Two hours later, the victim died. It was held that since the victim did not have a settled hopeless expectation of death at the time that he made his statement, the statement could not be admitted under this exception.

Not only are restrictive conditions imposed on the admissibility of dying declarations, the courts also impose restrictions on what may be said if the declaration is admitted. The general rule is that the dying declaration must be confined to the circumstances that led to the victim's death. On the other hand, a dying declaration is not only admissible against an accused, it also admissible in his favour. It is important therefore that everything that occurred immediately before and after the incident be allowed into evidence. Nevertheless, the court will impose certain restrictions. For example, in *Buck*[8] the accused was charged with manslaughter arising out of an illegal operation on a young girl. Although the court was prepared to allow a dying declaration as to what occurred at the time of the operation, it did not permit that part of her declaration which said that he attempted to procure an abortion on her some weeks before.

(ii) Declarations made in the Course of Duty

This exception to the hearsay rule allows the use of an oral or written record or statement made by a deceased person in the usual and ordinary course of his business. The theory here is that if an agent or servant routinely does something, it is likely to be accurate. Moreover, it is argued that an agent or servant has an interest in making an accurate record because his employer will probably keep a check upon its accuracy and fire him if it is not accurate.

One might seriously question whether these reasons are good enough to support this exception to the hearsay rule. We all know that people do make errors when they are making reports, and there

---

[7] *Supra*, note 5.
[8] (1940), 74 C.C.C. 314 (Ont. C.A.).

is no way of checking the accuracy of the record once it is admitted. There is also the possibility that an employee may be trying to cheat or defraud his employer. In such case, an innocent accused may discover that he has no way of attacking the record's accuracy. However, error or deliberate fraud are considered to be such rare occurrences in comparison to usual or customary conduct that it is felt to be in the public interest generally that the evidence be admitted.

Let us assume that Detective Jones sends out Officer Smith to make certain observations as to what is happening at the home of a suspect and to report to him. In due course, Officer Smith returns and reports his observations to Detective Jones. If Officer Smith dies before the case comes to trial, then what he observed and reported to Detective Jones may be repeated by him in court, if it was a report made in the usual and ordinary course of business. It is expected to be truthful and accurate because Jones will check upon its accuracy.

Let us take another example. It is well known that police officers, when conducting an investigation, make notes of everything that they observe in order to enable them to refresh their memories of the events when called upon to testify, days, weeks, months, or even years after the event. We assume that an officer would try to be as accurate and as comprehensive as he can be in the preparation of those notes. Should such notes be admitted in evidence if the police officer dies before the trial of the accused? It is arguable that the notes are made in the usual and ordinary course of business. However, the notes are for the officer's personal use. Unless he is required to file those notes with a superior officer who can check upon their accuracy, it cannot be said that it is unlikely that the notes will be false or inaccurate.

This common law exception must be distinguished from the provisions of sections 29 and 30 of the *Canada Evidence Act*.[9] Those sections permit any financial record (section 29) or business record (section 30) made in the usual or ordinary course of business to be admitted whether the person making them is dead or alive. A typical example involves a person's bank records. Let us assume that Mr. Smith purchased a television set with a cheque that was returned N.S.F. and was charged with either false pretences or fraud. To

9 R.S.C. 1985, c. C-5.

establish that Smith had insufficient funds in his account, and that in the course of his dealings with the bank, Smith never did put in sufficient monies to honour the cheque, the prosecution would have to produce his bank records. However, the bank records by themselves are hearsay. They are merely notations or records made by bank employees who dealt with Smith. Normally the prosecution would be required to call every employee of the bank who ever dealt with Smith to show what he deposited in his account or withdrew from it.

Section 29 of the *Act* allows the prosecution to introduce the record itself if it is established that at the time of making the entry, the record was one of the ordinary records of the bank, that the entry was made in the usual and ordinary course of business, that the record was in the custody or control of the bank, and that the copy is a true copy of the entry. Proof may be given by the manager or accountant of the bank, either orally or by affidavit. Section 30 further permits the introduction of a business record made in the usual and ordinary course of business provided that seven days notice is given before its production.[10]

(iii) Declarations against Interest

Another exception to the hearsay rule is a declaration against penal, pecuniary or proprietary interest. In other words, if someone says something which might effect his liberty, his pocket book, or his right or interest to certain property, what he says will be admitted in evidence if that person dies before he can be called upon to give evidence at trial. This was not always the rule. For a long time, only declarations affecting a person's pecuniary or proprietary interest, but not his penal interest, were admissible in court.[11] However, in 1977 the Supreme Court of Canada decided that it was only logical and proper that it should extend to a penal interest.[12] There Mr. Justice Dickson wrote,

> The effect of the rule in *The Sussex Peerage Case*, as it has been generally understood, is to render admissible the statement by a deceased that he received payment of a debt from another or that he held a parcel of land

---

[10] *Bicknell* (1988), 41 C.C.C. (3d) 546 (B.C. C.A.).
[11] *Sussex Peerage Case* (1844), 8 E.R. 1034.
[12] *O'Brien* (1977), 38 C.R.N.S. 325, 35 C.C.C. (2d) 209 (S.C.C.).

as a tenant and not an owner, but to render inadmissible a confession by a deceased that he and not someone else was the real perpetrator of the crime. The distinction is arbitrary and tenuous. There is little or no reason why declarations against penal interest and those against pecuniary or proprietary interests should not stand on the same footing. A person is as likely to speak the truth in a matter affecting his liberty as in a matter affecting his pocket book. For these reasons and the ever-present possibility that a rule of absolute prohibition could lead to grave injustice I would hold that, in a proper case, a declaration against penal interest is admissible according to the law of Canada; the rule as to absolute exclusion of declarations against penal interest, established in *The Sussex Peerage case*, should not be followed.

In the same year, the Supreme Court also endorsed the following test for determining what was a declaration against penal interest.[13]

1. The declaration must be made to a person in such circumstances that the declarant could be said to apprehend being vulnerable to penal consequences. For example, if one says something to a member of the family, such as a parent or a spouse, or even a child, one does not expect that person to report him to the police and expose him to the risk of prosecution.
2. The declarant's vulnerability to penal consequences must not be too remote. In other words, one must be able to say that the person who hears the declaration will probably inform the police and expose the declarant to prosecution.
3. Not every declaration which appears to be against penal interest will be admitted. The court must look at the totality of the words spoken and conclude that the whole tenor of the weight is against the declarant's penal interest.
4. In a doubtful case, the court must look at all of the circumstances and consider whether or not there is any other evidence connecting the declarant with the crime, and whether there is evidence connecting the declarant and the accused.

It is of significance to note that the Court also said that the exception was not restricted only to declarants since deceased. The declaration was admissible if the declarant was alive but unavailable to testify by reason of insanity, grave illness which prevented the giving of testimony even from a bed, or absence in a jurisdic-

---

[13] *Demeter* (1977), 38 C.R.N.S. 317, 34 C.C.C. (2d) 137 (S.C.C.).

tion where he could not be compelled by an order of the court to attend the accused's trial.

One can easily understand why the courts carefully scrutinize declarations against penal interest. Just as a person who is about to die may wish to settle an old score with an enemy by accusing him of a crime, a person about to die may wish to save a member of his family or a friend from prosecution by falsely confessing to the crime. The law does not accept the former as evidence unless it is a dying declaration. The latter is accepted because the consequences are less severe. The possibility of convicting an innocent man based on a false accusation of guilt is far worse than the acquittal of a person who might be guilty.

(iv) Declarations as to Physical or Mental Condition (State of Mind)

As was pointed out initially in this chapter, a statement is hearsay and excluded only when it is offered to prove a fact in issue. If, however, the statement is offered only to prove that the statement was made, it is not hearsay and is clearly admissible. This is what is known as original evidence. The failure to understand the difference between hearsay evidence and original evidence is a problem that frequently arises when one side seeks to call evidence of a statement or declaration made with respect to a physical or mental condition.

Let us take a simple example. X says to Y, "I am afraid because Z has threatened to kill me." X is subsequently found dead and Z is charged with his murder. Is the statement that X made to Y about his fear of Z admissible? It is a declaration as to a mental condition, namely, a fear. If the only purpose of admitting the statement is to show a fear, then it would be clearly admissible. In that sense it is original. What is objectionable are the words "because Z has threatened to kill me." If admitted, it would permit the jury to infer that X's fear of Z was justified. But without those added words, the declaration "I am afraid" standing alone would have no probative value. The judge has three options. The first is to exclude it altogether. The second is to admit only the statement "I am afraid." The third is to admit the entire statement and then to tell the jury that they should use it only as evidence of X's fear but not evidence that it was Z who was the cause of that fear.

Occasionally, the choices are not so straight forward. Take, for example, the decision of the Privy Council in *Ratten*.[14] Ratten was charged with the murder of his wife by deliberately shooting her. His defence was that he shot her accidentally. Shortly before her death, Mrs. Ratten made a telephone call and said "get me the police, please". Mr. Ratten denied that his wife ever made a telephone call. The trial judge allowed the telephone operator who had received that call to testify that she had received a telephone call, that the voice on the other end was hysterical and sobbing, and what the person said. It was held by the Privy Council that the evidence was relevant to prove the state of mind or emotion of Mrs. Ratten and to rebut the defence of accident.

Let us also look at a Canadian case, *Wysochan*.[15] There the issue was whether a woman was killed by her husband or by the accused. Each blamed the other. About a half an hour after the woman had been shot, her husband appeared on the scene and she stretched out her arms to him and said: "Stanley, help me out because there is a bullet in my body"; and later, "Stanley, help me. I am too hot." The Crown applied to have what she said admitted into evidence. The trial judge admitted her statements to show her state of mind. As he put it, "Would it not have been a most improbable thing had he (her husband) been the author of her death that night?"

One might ask, "What was the relevance of the statements in both cases?" In the *Ratten* case, the fact that the victim wanted the police was not relevant to the question of whether her death was deliberate or an accident. In *Wysochan*, the fact that the victim wanted her husband to help her or that she was too hot was not relevant as to who shot her. If the victim in each case had named her killer, then her statement would have been clearly hearsay and excluded unless it fell within one of the exceptions, such as a dying declaration or the *res gestae* (which will be discussed later). In both cases, the court held that it fell into neither exception.

In each case, the statement was admitted because it was a declaration as to the victim's physical or mental condition, even though her physical or mental condition was not a fact which the Crown was required to prove to establish its case against the accused. What the Crown had to establish was that a murder had been committed,

---

[14] (1971), 3 All E.R. 801, [1972] A.C. 378 (P.C.).
[15] (1930), 54 C.C.C. 172 (Sask. C.A.).

that the accused had committed it and that he had the requisite mental intent. Because in each case, the victim's statement was as to her physical or mental condition, the court said that it was original evidence as to that issue, not hearsay. However, by allowing the statement to be admitted as original evidence of the victim's state of mind, the court, in effect, also indirectly allowed it to be used for its hearsay content: in *Ratten*, to show that the killing was deliberate, not an accident; and, in *Wysochan*, to show that it was the accused and not the victim's husband who committed the murder.

(v) Declarations as to Intention

If A says to B that he intends to go and visit C and is later found dead outside C's residence, the logical inference is that he tried to carry out his intention. The rules of evidence will permit B to tell the court what he was told by A as evidence that A expressed an intention to visit C. However, what the common law has not permitted is the inference that A, in fact, met C where C is charged with causing the death of A, unless C was present when the statement was made.

One of the earliest cases dealing with this rule was an English case, *Wainwright*.[16] There Chief Justice Cockburn refused to admit a statement by the deceased victim that she intended to visit the accused. He ruled it out because "It was only a statement of intention which might or might not have been carried out." Although one might have thought that the concern of the Chief Justice should have been more with the question of weight rather than relevance, the view that such evidence is not admissible continues to influence Canadian authorities.

Some common law jurisdictions have gotten away from this restrictive view of such evidence. In *Walton*,[17] the High Court of Australia permitted evidence that the murder victim had stated that she intended to meet her husband (the accused) at the Town Centre, as evidence from which the jury could draw the inference that the two met at the appointed place. As Chief Justice Mason noted, ...

---

[16] (1975), 13 Cox C.C. 171.
[17] (1988), 84 A.L.R. 59 (H.C.), at p. 65.

her belief that she was to meet the applicant made it more probable that she travelled to the Town Centre.''

In fact, a century earlier, the Supreme Court of the United States was prepared to permit inferences to be drawn from a declarant's intention. In *Mutual Life Insurance Co. v. Hillmon*,[18] John Hillmon's wife had sued Mutual Life to recover on an insurance policy issued by Mutual Life on the life of her husband whose body had been found in Kansas. The defence was told that the body in the grave was not that of Hillmon but of one, Walters who had also disappeared and that he had been killed by Hillmon to allow Mrs. Hillmon to collect on the policy. The Supreme Court held that letters written by Walters to his sister indicating an intention to accompany Hillmon on a trip out west were admissible as evidence of his intention to go with Hillmon, "which made it more probable both that he did go and that he went with Hillmon".

Canadian courts, however, have continued to apply the strict common law rule. Recently, in *Smith*,[19] the Supreme Court of Canada considered the Hillmon case but decided to reject it in favour of the English position in *Kearley*.[20] In Smith, the victim of a murder had driven from Detroit to Canada with the accused where they spent the weekend together in a hotel. According to the theory of the Crown, the accused abandoned the victim at a hotel when she refused to take cocaine back to the United States and then picked her up and drove her to a service station where he strangled her. To support this theory, the Crown relied upon four telephone calls made by the victim to her mother discussing her association with the accused just before she was murdered. On the first two occasions, the victim told her mother that she had been abandoned at a hotel by the accused and needed transportation home. On the third occasion, she called her mother and said that the accused had just returned and she would not need a ride home after all. On the fourth occasion, she called and told her mother that she was on her way home. She was later found dead near the service station where she had made her last call.

The Ontario Court of Appeal held that the first two calls were admissible as statements of the victim's existing state of mind and of her intention to go home; they were not evidence that the accused

---

[18] 145 U.S. 285 (U.S. 1892).
[19] (1992), 15 C.R. (4th) 133, 75 C.C.C. (3d) 257 (S.C.C.).
[20] [1992] 2 All E.R. 345 (H.L.).

left her at the hotel. Although it was argued that the third call was evidence of the victim's state of mind and her intention to leave with the accused, from which it could be inferred that she did go with the accused, the Court held that it was not admissible to prove that the accused picked her up. The fourth call was also held inadmissible for the same reason. A further appeal to the Supreme Court of Canada was also dismissed. The Court agreed that a declaration of intention by the deceased could not be used to prove that someone other than the deceased probably acted in accordance with that intention.

In summary then, Canadian authority does not permit B to tell the court that A told him that he was going to visit C for the purpose of drawing the inference that he probably met C. But there is no prohibition against B stating that A told him that he intended to visit C as evidence of his personal intention to visit C. If, for example, the fact in issue is whether C killed A, what is frowned upon is allowing B to tell the court that A told him that he intended to visit C for the purpose of inferring that A probably met C. The reason is that it would permit the trier to infer that A and C must have met and that C caused A's death. The difficulty is that once the evidence is introduced, it would be difficult for the jury not to draw that inference even if they were instructed not to do so by the judge.

(b) Some Assertions of Living Persons

(i) Co-conspirators

Where an accused is charged with the crime of conspiracy to commit an illegal act, proof that he agreed to commit the illegal act is sufficient to obtain a conviction. It is not necessary for the prosecution to prove that the accused also committed the illegal act which the conspirators planned to commit. But proving a conspiracy is generally very difficult because such agreements are usually made in secret and the only witnesses present are the conspirators themselves. Thus an exception to the hearsay rule has developed which allows the prosecution to prove the conspiracy by introducing evidence of the acts and declarations of fellow members of the conspiracy, performed and made in pursuance of the objects of the conspiracy.

This exception is very confusing because it first requires proof of membership in the conspiracy by direct evidence other than hearsay before the acts and declarations of co-conspirators may be introduced. However, this initial proof of membership need only be made on a balance of probabilities. Once proof has been established, then the hearsay exception kicks in and the prosecution is allowed to introduce evidence of acts and declarations of co-conspirators to prove the conspiracy beyond a reasonable doubt.

In practice what happens is that all of the evidence (including the hearsay) is admitted and at the conclusion of the case, the trial judge is required to instruct the jury (or himself where trial is by judge alone) that they must conduct their deliberations in two stages. They must first look at only the direct evidence of membership and determine whether the accused is probably a member of the conspiracy. If they are satisfied that he is, then and only then are they allowed to consider the hearsay evidence in determining whether proof has been established beyond a reasonable doubt.[21]

(ii) Identification Parades

Where a fact in issue is the identity of the perpetrator of the crime, it is necessary for the prosecutor to ask a witness who can identify the person to point him out to the jury. A typical question is "Do you see the person who ... in this courtroom?". This is usually not very difficult because the accused will be sitting by himself (or with a co-accused) in the prisoner's dock.

However, those involved in the administration of justice know from experience that the identification of an accused for the first time in the prisoner's dock is notoriously suspect and can lead to a miscarriage of justice. The ordinary juror on the other hand may not be aware of this. For this reason, an exception to the hearsay rule has developed which permits police officers, or anyone else who is present when a prior identification is made by a witness, to give evidence not only that the witness identified the accused but also of the surrounding circumstances of that identification. For example, the officer who was present during an identification parade (a lineup) or when a witness was shown a photo-lineup, or when a composite drawing was prepared is entitled to give evidence that

---

[21] *Carter* (1982), 31 C.R. (3d) 97, 67 C.C.C. (2d) 568 (S.C.C.).

the witness identified a particular person in the lineup or the composite drawing, whether or not the witness hesitated before making the identification, what words the witness used in making the identification, etc. Such evidence will give the trier of fact a complete picture of all of the surrounding circumstances which led to the accused's ultimate identification in the prisoner's dock and will enable the trier to properly assess the value of that identification.[22]

When a police officer or other person in attendance at the identification gives evidence of a prior identification by the witness, it is said to be original evidence not hearsay. It is original evidence because the officer is only saying that the witness identified a certain person, not that the person is the one who committed the offence. However, that distinction is really misleading. It allows, in effect, the trier of fact to infer from the officer's testimony that since the witness identified him, that person must be the one who committed the crime.

(iii) Recent Developments

Historically, exceptions to the hearsay rule have only been allowed where the speaker is dead and therefore unable to testify. However, in recent years the Supreme Court has decided that the hearsay rule should be relaxed and hearsay statements admitted even where the declarant is alive but is unable for some reason to come to the court to testify. One decision discussed earlier is *O'Brien*.[23] There Chief Justice Dickson of the Supreme Court of Canada suggested that declarations against penal interest may be admitted where the declarant is unavailable to testify by reason of insanity, grave illness or absence from the jurisdiction of Canadian courts.

The first Canadian decision to relax the rigidity of the hearsay rule was an Alberta case, *Ares v. Venner*,[24] dealing with declarations made in the course of duty is. In that case, the plaintiff, who had fractured his leg while skiing, had sued the doctor who had reduced the fracture and applied a plaster cast for not removing the cast in time to prevent muscle necrosis from a lack of blood supply. As a result, the plaintiff's leg had to be amputated below

---

[22] *Langille* (1990), 59 C.C.C. (3d) 544 (Ont. C.A.); *McCay* (1990), 91 Cr.App.R. 84 (C.A.).
[23] *Supra*, note 12.
[24] (1970), 12 C.R.N.S. 349 (S.C.C.).

the knee. The issue before the court was whether records kept by nurses at the hospital were admissible to show their observations of the pulse, temperature and condition of the plaintiff. Alberta at that time had no provision, similar to that of other provinces, such as Ontario, allowing the admission of medical records of a patient. Although the nurses who made the records were alive and were, in fact, waiting outside the courtroom to testify, the plaintiff had not called them but had been permitted by the trial judge to introduce the nurse's notes. The Supreme Court of Canada held that such records were admissible as declarations made in the ordinary course of duty and were "*prima facie* proof of the facts stated therein" even though the nurses were available to give oral testimony.

In reaching that conclusion, the Court rejected the decision of the House of Lords in *Myers v. D.P.P.*,[25] where it was held that judges should not re-state the law to meet modern conditions but should leave it to Parliament to do the job. Ironically, it was not really necessary for the Supreme Court to have extended the rule at all. The issue in *Ares v. Venner*[26] was whether the doctor was negligent in failing to remove the cast from the plaintiff's leg after he had read the nurse's notes which described the plaintiff's condition (i.e., toes were swollen, numb, blue etc.), not whether the contents of the notes were correct. In other words, had the nurse's notes been admitted, not as proof of the contents, but to show that the doctor should have been alerted by what he read in those notes to look at the plaintiff's leg, no hearsay problem would have arisen.

Twenty years later, the Supreme Court of Canada relied on *Ares v. Venner* to approve the reception of statements made by children to others about sexual abuse provided that the twin requirements of "necessity" and "reliability" had been met. In *Khan*,[27] Madame Justice McLachlin delivering the judgment of the Court noted that Canadian law was moving towards a more flexible attitude in the reception of the hearsay evidence of children, particularly where the statement concerns sexual abuse. In that case, a 3 1/2 year old child had been examined privately in the office of Dr. Khan, a medical doctor. After the examination, the child's mother had noticed a wet spot on the sleeve of her daughter's clothing.

---

[25] [1964] 2 All E.R. 881.
[26] *Supra*, note 24.
[27] (1990), 79 C.R. (3d) 1 (S.C.C.).

About ten to fifteen minutes after the mother and daughter left Khan's office, they had a conversation about the visit and the child described an incident that could amount to a sexual abuse.

Madame Justice McLachlin found the requirement of "necessity" in the fact that unless admitted, the child's evidence would be inadmissible, and to require the child to testify would be traumatic to her. She found the requirement of "reliability" in the fact that the child had no motive to falsify her story, which emerged naturally and without prompting, and the fact that she could not have knowledge of such sexual acts. She also noted that the child's statement was corroborated by real evidence.

Following the *Khan* decision, it was naturally assumed by the trial courts that if the infant could testify, then the element of necessity no longer existed and the hearsay declaration was not admissible. Indeed, when Dr. Khan was re-tried, the victim was now 9 years old and found competent by the trial judge to testify. Since she was competent to testify, the trial judge held that her statement to her mother was now inadmissible because there was no longer any necessity for it.

Although a child may be competent to testify, he or she may be unable to express herself with frankness, accuracy, fullness or candidness. The result may be that unless the child's out-of-court statement is admitted, despite her legal competency, the child's version of the events may not be adequately placed before the trier of fact. This was recognized by the Ontario Court of Appeal in *College of Physicians v. Khan*,[28] a case involving Dr. Khan's discipline proceedings before the Ontario College of Physicians. There the Ontario Court of Appeal held that the Supreme Court's decision in *Khan* did not preclude the admission of the hearsay statement even when the child testifies. Mr. Justice Doherty delivering the judgment of the Court wrote,

> In my view, if that tribunal is satisfied that despite the viva voce evidence of the child, it is still 'reasonably necessary' to admit the out-of-court statement in order to obtain an accurate and frank rendition of the child's version of the relevant events, then the necessity criterion set down in *Khan* is satisfied.[29]

---

[28] (1992), 76 C.C.C. (3d) 10 (Ont. C.A.).
[29] *Supra*, note 27 at p. 24.

Recently, the Supreme Court of Canada has said that the hearsay rule should no longer preclude the reception of evidence which does not fall within old established categories of exceptions. In *Smith*,[30] the Court held that hearsay evidence of statements made by persons who are not available to give evidence at trial ought generally to be admissible where the circumstances under which the statements are made to satisfy the criteria of necessity and reliability set out in *Khan* and subject to the residual discretion of the trial judge to exclude the evidence where its probative value is slight and undue prejudice may result to the accused.

An extension of this new rule had been recognized earlier by the British Columbia Court of Appeal in *Chahley*.[31] There the accused, who was charged with murder by slitting the deceased's throat, had sought unsuccessfully at trial to adduce evidence of statements made by the deceased to his common law wife several days before his death to the effect that a black man had pulled a knife on him and he couldn't go downtown for a while. In fact, the deceased had remained in his apartment for several days until he received a telephone call and had left telling his common law wife that "everything's okay now". It was held that since the statements met the twin tests of necessity and reliability, they should have been admitted as evidence for their truth to support the accused's defence that the murder had been committed by someone else. Necessity was met since the declarant was dead. The test of reliability was met because the statements made by the declarant were not in favour of his interest, were made before dispute or litigation and the declarant had the peculiar means of knowledge not possessed in ordinary cases.

This rapid acceleration by the Supreme Court in relaxing the rigidity of the hearsay rule has raised a number of problems for trial judges. For example, what does "necessity" mean. In *S.(K.O.)*,[32] Mr. Justice Wetmore interpreted the word "necessity" in the context of the *Khan* case to have a two-fold meaning. The evidence had to be necessary in the sense of being crucial to the case. But his view that it also had to be "reasonably necessary" in the sense that direct evidence was not available, was rejected by

---

[30] (1992), 15 C.R. (4th) 133, 75 C.C.C. (3d) 257 (S.C.C.).
[31] (1992), 72 C.C.C. (3d) 193 (B.C. C.A.).
[32] (1991), 4 C.R. (4th) 37, 63 C.C.C. (3d) 91 (B.C.S.C.).

the Ontario Court of Appeal in *College of Physicians v. Khan.*[33] There, as has already been noted, the Court decided that it was "reasonably necessary" to admit an out-of-court statement, in addition to direct evidence, in order to obtain an accurate and frank rendition of the child's version of the events.

The requirement of "reliability" creates more difficulty for the courts. Obviously, it is not necessary for the Crown to satisfy the trial judge that the words uttered are true beyond a reasonable doubt. If it were required to do so, then there would be no necessity for a trial. There must, however, be some threshold test that will show a degree of persuasiveness that the statement could be found truthful when weighed along with the other evidence.

Two considerations have received recent judicial approval. The first is the reliability of the declarant and the witness; the second is the circumstances under which the statement was made. Both considerations were applied by the Supreme Court of Canada in *Smith.*[34] There the victim of a murder had driven from Detroit to Canada with the accused where they spent the weekend together in a hotel. According to the theory of the Crown, the accused abandoned the victim at a hotel when she refused to take cocaine back to the United States and then picked her up and drove her to a service station where he strangled her. To support this theory, the Crown relied upon four telephone calls made by the victim to her mother discussing her association with the accused. On the first two occasions, the victim told her mother that she had been abandoned at a hotel by the accused and needed transportation home. On the third occasion, she called her mother and said that the accused had just returned and she would not need a ride home after all. On the fourth occasion, she called and told her mother that she was on her way home. She was later found dead near the service station where she made her last call. The Supreme Court of Canada concluded that the first two calls had the necessary indicia of reliability because there was no known reason for the victim to lie. The court rejected the third telephone call because the circumstances under which it was made were such that the victim might have been mistaken or might have intended to deceive her mother.

A further consideration which has been dealt with at the trial

---

[33] *Supra*, note 28.
[34] *Supra*, note 30.

level is whether "other evidence" in the case may be used to support the reliability of the statement. In *Stark*,[35] Mr. Justice Glithero admitted the utterance of the deceased to her female friend that she intended to meet the accused for lunch. In considering the reliability of the statement, he noted that the accused denied any meeting to the police but admitted to his wife and mother that he met the deceased for lunch. There seems to be no logical reason why such "other evidence" should not be considered in determining the reliability of the statement. What seems to be clear from the authorities is that rarely will an out-of court-statement be admitted where it is the only evidence against the accused.

(c) Res Gestae

The term *"res gestae"* is a Latin phrase that is too often used and misused by judges and lawyers. Professor Wigmore called it useless "because every rule of Evidence to which it has ever been applied exists as a part of some other well established principle and can be explained in the terms of that principle." He also called it harmful "because by its ambiguity it invites the confusion of one rule with another and thus creates uncertainty as to the limitations of both." He suggested that it should be wholly repudiated. Regrettably, judges and lawyers continue to use it more than ever.

The rule has been expressed this way,

> Acts, declarations, and incidents which constitute, or accompany and explain, the fact or transaction in issue, are admissible, for or against either party, as forming part of the res gestae.[36]

In *Teper*,[37] Lord Normand attempted to justify the reception of evidence which forms part of the *res gestae* this way,

> It appears to rest ultimately on two propositions, that human utterance is both a fact and a means of communication, and that human action may be so interwoven with words that the significance of the action cannot be understood without the correlative words, and the dissociation of the words from the action would impede the discovery of truth.

---

[35] (August, 1994), Glithero J. (Ont. Gen. Div.).
[36] Phipson on Evidence (11th ed.), para. 171.
[37] [1952] A.C. 480.

The above passages speak of *res gestae* as being words which give significance to or explain conduct or action. In *Bedingfield*,[38] discussed earlier, the victim, who was Bedingfield's mistress, came out of a room where Bedingfield was subsequently found, pointed to her throat which was cut and said to one of her assistants "see what Harry has done". She died ten minutes later. Bedingfield's first name was Harry. The trial judge, Chief Justice Cockburn, would not permit the statement to be admitted in evidence because the transaction, that is the cutting of her throat, was over and completed when she made the statement. Later decisions accepted this restriction and argued that a statement or declaration could not be admitted as part of the *res gestae* unless it accompanied the act and explained it.

Professor Wigmore strongly criticized this restriction. He argued that it arose out of a failure to understand the distinction between what may be described as a verbal act and a spontaneous exclamation. A verbal act is simply words which accompany an act and explain it. As Wigmore pointed out,

> Without the words, the act as a whole may be incomplete; and until the words are taken into consideration, the desired significance can not be attributed to the wordless conduct.[39]

Without the accompanying words, the act has no significance. The words explain the act. This means that when a witness who has seen the act and heard the accompanying words testifies as to what he has seen and heard, he is giving first-hand or original evidence, not second-hand evidence. In other words, it is not an exception to the hearsay rule because it is not hearsay at all. This means that res gestae is not, in a strict sense, an exception to the hearsay rule. It allows the admission of statements which would otherwise be hearsay to explain conduct or actions which might otherwise be ambiguous.

Professor Wigmore, however, argued that spontaneous exclamations ought to be admitted as an exception to the hearsay rule. His reasons were these,

> Under certain external circumstances of physical shock, a stress of nervous excitement may be produced which stills the reflective faculties and removes

---

[38] (1879), 14 Cox 341.
[39] *Supra*, note 1 at p. 267.

their control, so that the utterance which then occurs is a spontaneous and sincere response to the actual sensations and perceptions already produced by the external shock. Since this utterance is made under the immediate and uncontrolled domination of the senses, and during the brief period when considerations of self interest could not have been brought fully to bear by reasoned reflection, the utterance may be taken as particularly trustworthy, (or, at least, as lacking the usual grounds of untrustworthiness), and thus as expressing the real tenor of the speaker's belief as to the facts just observed by him; and may therefore be received as testimony to those facts.[40]

If we might use the *Bedingfield*[41] case as an example, Professor Wigmore would argue that Bedingfield's mistress' exclamation as to "what Harry has done" was "a spontaneous and sincere response to the actual sensations and perceptions already produced by the external shock" of having her throat cut. It was also made "during the brief period when considerations of self interest could not have been brought fully to bear by reasoned reflection." Thus, he would argue that the utterance should be taken as particularly trustworthy and should be admitted as an exception to the hearsay rule.

For almost seventy years, *Bedingfield* was religiously followed by Canadian and English courts. In 1950, there was some attempt to introduce the concept of "spontaneous exclamation" in an Ontario case but it was quickly rejected. In *Leland*,[42] the accused and her husband were jointly charged with manslaughter arising out of the stabbing of one, Monteith, in whose house both were residing as roomers. During a quarrel between Monteith and the accused's husband, all of the lights in the house were turned off. When the lights were turned on again, Monteith was heard to say to his wife "Rose, she stabbed me" and died a few minutes later. Monteith's wife's name was Rose. The trial judge admitted the statement without specifically referring to it as a "spontaneous exclamation." However, the Ontario Court of Appeal said that he was wrong to do so because "our rules of evidence do not seem to extend to cover a case of spontaneous exclamation, in the broad terms stated by Wigmore." Nor was the Court prepared to admit it as part of the *res gestae* because,

---

[40] *Supra*, note 1, Vol. 6, para 1747, at p. 195.
[41] *Supra*, note 38.
[42] (1950), 11 C.R. 152, 98 C.C.C. 337 (Ont. C.A.).

The fight had ceased. No one was pursuing the deceased or seeking to continue the struggle.[43]

However, in 1972 the House of Lords in *Ratten*,[44] concluded that the *Bedingfield* rule was too restrictive. In *Ratten*, the Crown sought to introduce the evidence of a telephone operator who had received a telephone call from the deceased's home 10 minutes before she was shot. The call came from a woman who sounded hysterical and who said "get me the police, please" — gave her address but before a connection was made, hung up. The trial judge admitted the statement. Lord Wilberforce, delivering the judgment of the House, said that he was correct in doing so. It was his view that the admissibility of such statements did not depend on there being exact contemporaneity with the act to be explained.

> ...hearsay evidence may be admitted if the statement providing it is made in such conditions (always being those of approximate but not exact contemporaneity) of involvement or pressure as to exclude the possibility of concoction or distortion to the advantage of the maker or the disadvantage of the accused.[45]

The test which the trial judge had to apply was whether there was the possibility of concoction or fabrication, not whether the statement was part of the event or transaction.

> ... if the drama, leading up to the climax, has commenced and assumed such intensity and pressure that the utterance can safely be regarded as a true reflection of what was unrolling or actually happening, it ought to be received.[46]

Ratten was re-affirmed 14 years later by the House of Lords in *Blastland*[47] and again, a year later, by the House of Lords in *Andrews*.[48] In *Andrews*, *Bedingfield* was specifically overruled.

The concept of "spontaneous exclamation" espoused by Wigmore and the relaxation of the narrow "exact contemporaneity" test of *Bedingfield* was finally accepted by the Ontario Court of

---

[43] *Ibid.*
[44] *Supra*, note 14.
[45] *Supra*, note 14 at p. 391 (A.C.).
[46] *Supra*, note 14 at p. 390 (A.C.).
[47] [1986] A.C. 41.
[48] [1987] 1 A.C. 281.

Appeal in *Clark*.[49] There it was held that the evidence of a witness that she heard the victim yell, "Help! Help! I've been murdered! I've been stabbed!" was admissible as a spontaneous statement made in circumstances as to exclude the possibility of concoction or distortion. The statements were contemporaneous with the unfolding events even though they did not accompany the actual stabbing.

However, in *Kahn*[50] the Supreme Court of Canada cast doubt upon the correctness of *Clark* by re-affirming that the traditional tests of contemporaneity and pressure or emotional intensity must exist before a hearsay statement will be admitted under this exception. There, a 3 1/2 year old child had been examined privately by Dr. Khan, a medical doctor. About 10 to 15 minutes after they left Khan's office, the child described to her mother an incident that took place in his office that could amount to a sexual assault. The mother was not allowed by the trial judge to repeat what her daughter told her because it was not, in his opinion, a spontaneous utterance. The Court of Appeal in *Khan*, however, disagreed.[51] Mr. Justice Robins wrote,

> The time that may elapse before a statement following an event capable of rendering it spontaneous is rendered inadmissible will depend on a variety of factors. These include, for instance, the nature and circumstances of the act or event, the nature and circumstances of the statement, the place where the event occurred or the statement was made, the possible influence of intervening events, and the condition and age of the declarant. Each case must depend on its own circumstances; no two cases are identical, and the exact length of time is not subject to mathematical measurement. In any given case, the ultimate question is whether the statement relating to the alleged startling event was made near enough in time to the event to exclude any realistic opportunity for fabrication or concoction.

But Madame Justice McLachlin, delivering the judgment of the Supreme Court of Canada, held that the trial judge was correct in rejecting the statement as a spontaneous utterance because it was neither contemporaneous nor made under pressure or emotional intensity. She was not prepared to relax the strict requirements as to the admissibility of a spontaneous utterance, as had been done in the United States, particularly in cases of sex offences against children. It was her concern that admissibility under this

---

[49] (1983), 35 C.R. (2d) 357, 7 C.C.C. (3d) 46 (Ont. C.A.).
[50] *Supra*, note 27.
[51] *Supra*, note 28.

exception to the hearsay rule did not impose the twin conditions of necessity and reliability before such utterances could be received. She preferred to admit such utterances only where they met those requirements that had been early imposed by the Supreme Court in *Ares v. Venner* discussed earlier.[52]

(d) Statutory Exceptions

As noted earlier, some statutes permit the introduction of hearsay evidence by affidavit or certificate where it would be inconvenient or even impossible to call the witness who is able to give direct evidence of the fact in issue. Let us assume for example that what has to be established is that X made certain deposits and withdrawals from his account at the Bank of Montreal. A strict application of the hearsay rule would require each bank teller who dealt with X to come forward and give evidence of that specific transaction. But we know that it would be unlikely that any of the tellers would remember the details of those transactions.

Section 29(1) of the *Act*, however, authorizes either the Crown or defence to introduce proof of those transactions by production of "a copy of any entry in any book or record kept in any financial institution" notwithstanding that the copy of the entry, or even the actual entry itself is, in a strict sense, hearsay. But before a copy of the entry is admitted, section 29(2) requires that certain conditions be established. Those conditions are considered crucial to the twin tests of necessity and reliability or trustworthiness discussed earlier. They include the requirement that the book or record be one of the ordinary books or records of the financial institution, that the entry was made in the usual and ordinary course of business, that the book or record be in the custody or control of the financial institution and that the copy be a true copy of the book or record. Where these conditions are established, proof of the entry may be given by the bank manager or the accountant, either orally or by affidavit. Similar provisions are contained in section 26 of the *Act* dealing with Government of Canada records and in section 30 with respect to business records.

Another common exception to the hearsay rule is section 9(1)

---

[52] *Supra*, note 24.

of the *Narcotic Control Act*.[53] It authorizes the results of the analysis of a substance suspected to be a narcotic to be given by a certificate purporting to be signed by a qualified analyst, provided that the other side has been given reasonable notice of the intention to rely on certificate evidence together with a copy of the certificate. Section 9(2) does, however, give the court the right to order the attendance of the analyst for the purpose of cross-examination.

---

[53] R.S.C. 1985, c. N-1.

4

Previous Consistent Statements

1. THE RULE

The general rule at common law is that a witness may not be asked in chief whether he previously made a statement consistent with his present testimony. For example, the prosecutor is not entitled to ask the victim of an assault whether she made a statement to the police consistent with her present testimony; nor may any other prosecution witness be permitted to repeat the victim's prior consistent statement. When it comes to the defence, there are two aspects of this rule. The first is that the defence is not allowed to call the accused or any other witness to testify that the accused made a statement before trial declaring his innocence. Secondly, the defence is not allowed to ask a prosecution witness during cross-examination about any statement made by the accused declaring his innocence.[1]

The rule, often called the rule against self-serving evidence, explains one of the reasons for it. It is to prevent witnesses, particularly an accused, from manufacturing or inventing evidence which serves their interests. It is only human nature for a jury to believe that because a victim previously declared the accused's guilt or an accused protested his innocence before trial, that evidence must be

---

[1] *Campbell* (1977), 1 C.R. (3d) 309, 38 C.C.C. (2d) 6 (Ont. C.A.).

true. It is for this reason that an accused is not entitled to lead evidence that he offered to take a polygraph test to demonstrate his innocence but his offer was refused by the police.[2] The purpose of the rule is to prevent the jury from being swayed by this side issue.

A good example of the rule is the *Roberts* case.[3] Roberts was charged with the murder of his girl friend. His defence was that he had shot her accidently while they were making up after a quarrel. Two days after the shooting, he told his father that his defence was that the shooting had been an accident. His father was not permitted to give evidence of that conversation because it was self-serving.

Instances where a prior consistent statement has been rejected by the courts are usually where the statement was made after the event. Nevertheless, if the purpose of the rule is to prevent a witness or an accused from contriving evidence to serve their interest, then it would follow that any statement made either before or after the event should be rejected. Unfortunately, a strict application of the rule may seem illogical where it is clear on the evidence that there was no possibility of contrivance. For example, in *Ferguson*[4] the issue was the identity of the person with whom the complainant said she had sexual intercourse twenty years before. The accused had not only denied that he had intercourse with the complainant but the fact that he even knew her. However, although the trial judge was satisfied that the contents of a letter sent by the complainant to a friend before the event identifying the accused as one with whom she had a developed a friendship could not, in the circumstances, have been manufactured, he felt that he was bound by authority not to admit it.

Another reason for the rule, particularly where it affects the defence, is to prevent an accused from avoiding the witness box by having someone else advance his defence. If the accused wishes to tell his story of what happened, he must do so by entering the witness box where he will be required to testify under oath and to subject himself to cross-examination.

However, the rule will not apply where the prosecution chooses to make the accused's explanation part of its case. For example, if the Crown decides, for whatever reason, to introduce the accused's statement at trial, it will be admissible even if it is self-serving. It

---

[2] *Beland* (1987), 60 C.R. (3d) 1, 36 C.C.C. (3d) 481 (S.C.C.).
[3] (1942), 28 Cr.App.R. 102.
[4] (June 8, 1994), Salhany J. (Ont. Gen. Div.).

is only where the defence attempts to introduce such evidence that the rule steps in to prevent it.

(2) Exceptions to the Rule

(a) To Rebut the Suggestion of Recent Fabrication

There are undoubtedly instances where prior consistent statements should be admitted. The first is where the defence suggests that the prosecution witness is testifying to events which one would have expected him or her to have mentioned at an earlier time, or where the prosecution suggests that the defence was recently invented or contrived. Here, it is only fair that the Crown or defence be allowed to rebut that suggestion by leading evidence that the witness's evidence or the accused's defence has been consistent throughout.[5] At the same time, the judge must remind the jury (or himself) of the limited use of such evidence. It can only be used to rebut the suggestion of recent fabrication or concoction. It must not be used as proof of its contents or to confirm the testimony of the witness being impeached.[6]

As a practical matter, the suggestion that the defence was recently invented or contrived will not arise very often because of an accused's right to remain silent. It would be very unfortunate if police officers were required to warn an accused of his right to remain silent and then be allowed to use that silence to complain of recent fabrication when the defence is revealed for the first time at trial. However, an exception will arise where the defence is alibi. Here, it is generally prudent for the defence to give the prosecution particulars of that alibi at the earliest opportunity.[7]

The usual time that the defence will suggest that a victim recently fabricated her complaint against the accused is during the course of the cross-examination of that victim. However, the

---

[5] *Garofoli* (1988), 64 C.R. (3d) 193, 41 C.C.C. (3d) 103 (Ont. C.A.), reversed on other grounds (1990), 80 C.R. (3d) 317, 60 C.C.C. (3d) 161 (S.C.C.); *Campbell* (1977) 1 C.R. (3d) 309, 38 C.C.C. (2d) 6 (Ont. C.A.).

[6] *Collins* (1992), 9 C.R. (4th) 377 (Ont. C.A.); *F. (J.E.)* (1994), 26 C.R. (4th) 220, 85 C.C.C. (3d) 457 (Ont. C.A.).

[7] *Robertson* (1975), 29 C.R.N.S. 141, 21 C.C.C. (2d) 385 (Ont. C.A.), leave to appeal to S.C.C. refused (1975), 21 C.C.C. (2d) 385n (S.C.C.).

suggestion need not be raised only at that time. In *Campbell*,[8] the Ontario Court of Appeal noted that,

> ...an express allegation of recent fabrication in cross-examination is not neces-sary before the exception, with respect to rebutting an allegation of recent fabrication, becomes operative, and that a suggestion that the accused's story has been recently contrived may also arise implicitly from the whole circum-stances of the case, the evidence of the witnesses who have been called and the conduct of the trial.

However, it has also been recognized that a prior consistent statement should not be admitted under the guise of recent fabri-cation unless the door is clearly opened.[9] But it may be opened by an opening statement of the defence, or through cross-examination of the complainant or other Crown witnesses, or by the allegation of recent fabrication becoming implicit from the defence's conduct of the case.

Once the suggestion of recent fabrication is raised, the Crown is required to apply to the court to be allowed to lead the evidence. If the trial judge is satisfied, after hearing submissions from both sides, that there has been a clear suggestion of recent fabrication by the defence, then the Crown will be entitled to lead the evidence through its witnesses. The same procedure will apply where the Crown has made a similar suggestion about the defence.

(b) To Show Consistency of Identification

The rule preventing the admissibility of a prior consistent state-ment is regularly breached in cases where the identification of the accused is in dispute. Evidence by a witness that the person stand-ing in the prisoner's dock "is the man" is generally regarded as valueless because it is open to "honest mistake and self-deception".[10]

Therefore, if the prosecution is relying on eye-witness identifi-cation, the police will usually attempt, in the initial stages of the investigation, to have the witness view a series of photographs or attend a lineup. The purpose is to see if the witness is able to pick out the suspected offender from the photographs or the lineup, with-

---

[8] *Supra*, note 5 at p. 325 (C.R.).
[9] *Owens* (1986), 55 C.R. (3d) 386, 33 C.C.C. (3d) 275 (Ont. C.A.).
[10] *Browne* (1951), 99 C.C.C. 141 (B.C. C.A.).

out any suggestion by the police. When the matter goes to trial, the witness will then be able to testify that he was shown a series of photographs or attended a lineup and picked out the accused without prompting.

Where the witness gives such evidence at trial, he is, in effect, giving evidence of his own prior consistent statement. Similarly, police officers present at the out-of-court identification are regularly allowed to testify that the witness viewed a series of photographs or attended a lineup and picked out the accused. When they do so, they are giving essentially hearsay evidence.[11] The officers, however, are not restricted to merely testifying that the witness identified a particular person or photograph. They are also entitled to give evidence as to all of the relevant circumstances surrounding the identification. Indeed, the defence will usually wish to cross-examine the officers on the surrounding circumstances to show that the witness may have hesitated before making the identification or was uncertain about it, in order to persuade the trier of fact that not much weight should be given to the evidence.

(c) As Part of the Res Gestae

Although *res gestae*, discussed earlier, is commonly linked with the hearsay rule, it is also an exception to the rule against previous consistent statements. Thus an exculpatory statement which is part of the *res gestae* may be admitted even though it self-serving. The theory is that a self-serving statement which is uttered contemporaneously with and explanatory of the act is unlikely to be contrived or manufactured.

For example, in *Graham*,[12] a majority panel of the Supreme Court of Canada held that the explanation given by an accused when first found in possession of stolen property was admissible as part of the *res gestae*. The rational for the decision was that the explanation given at the moment of discovery, if the same as that given at trial, was strong proof of the consistency of the accused's evidence.

---

[11] *Langille* (1990), 59 C.C.C. (3d) 544 (Ont. C.A.).
[12] (1972), 19 C.R.N.S. 117, 7 C.C.C. (2d) 93 (S.C.C.).

(d) To Rebut the Presumption of Consent in Sexual Assaults

At common law, the fact that a complaint was made by the victim of a sexual assault, but not what she actually said, was admissible at the trial of her attacker to show consistency in the victim's testimony. This rule developed from the ancient requirement that the victim of an attack should raise the hue and cry if a prosecution of rape was to succeed. It was based on the belief and presumption that a woman who did not complain of rape at the earliest opportunity must have consented to intercourse. The fact of the complaint, so long as it was made at the earliest opportunity, was admitted to show that the victim acted as one would normally expect her to do after a sexual attack. It allowed the judge and jury to infer that her consistency in repeating the same story at trial that she did after her attack was because she was a credible person.

Initially, the rule only allowed the fact of the complaint to be admitted but not what the victim actually said. Eventually, in *Lillyman*,[13] what the victim actually said was admitted although the jury were instructed that it was only relevant to show consistency in her conduct, presumably as a vain effort to avoid the rule against self-serving testimony.

Not surprisingly, this archaic rule was finally abrogated by Parliament in 1983. Its abolition does not mean that a complaint by a victim of a sexual assault is no longer admissible; it only means that there is no longer a presumption of consent which must be rebutted by evidence of a complaint. And if there is no presumption of consent, then there is no necessity for the Crown to lead evidence of a complaint in chief. However, if the defence suggests that the allegation of sexual assault was recently concocted, the prosecution will be allowed to lead evidence that the complaint was made at an earlier time to meet that suggestion. At the same time, the defence will be permitted to bring out the particulars of the prior complaint where it wishes to show that it is inconsistent with the complainant's testimony at trial.

(e) As Part of the Narrative

Victims of an offence are routinely permitted to give evidence that they complained to the police. Similarly, the police are per-

---

13 [1896] 2 Q.B. 167.

mitted to say that the victim made a complaint to them about a certain matter and they proceeded to investigate the complaint. Such evidence is technically a prior consistent statement but is admitted, not to show a consistency of conduct, but simply as part of the narrative. In other words, it is admitted by the court simply to show the sequence of events leading up to how the police became involved in the investigation.

However, the admission of a complaint by a victim under this exception has not been restricted to a complaint to the police. For example, in *George*,[14] a fourteen year old girl complained to her grandmother and her parents that her cousin had sexual intercourse with her without her consent. The cousin was then confronted with the allegation and admitted that it was true and that he was sorry. When the defence suggested to the girl in cross-examination that she had consented but changed her mind overnight, the trial judge permitted the Crown to call her grandmother, the girl's father and a doctor who had examined her to say what she had told them about what had happened.

Mr. Justice MacFarlane, who delivered the judgment of the British Columbia Court of Appeal, was of the view that the fact of the complaint, but not the contents, was admissible not to show consistency in conduct but as part of the narrative. In other words it was to show the sequence of events beginning with the complaint to the grandmother who in turn confronted the accused with the allegation. A similar view was expressed by the same Court in *Beliveau*.[15]

As in the case of the other exceptions to the rule against prior consistent statements, the trial judge is required to explain to the jury about the limited value of the evidence. They must be told that the statement is only admissible to show the sequence of events from the offence to the prosecution so that they can understand the conduct of the victim and assess the victim's truthfulness. They must also be told that they are not to look at the contents of the statement as proof that a crime has been committed.[16]

---

[14] (1985), 23 C.C.C. (3d) 42 (B.C. C.A.).
[15] (1986), 30 C.C.C. (3d) 193 (B.C. C.A.).
[16] *F. (J.E.)*, *supra*, note 6.

(f) Answers of An Accused When Taxed With The Situation

If the reason for excluding a prior consistent statement of an accused is to prevent him or her from manufacturing or inventing a defence, one might ask why a statement by an accused when taxed with the situation either by a policeman or someone else is not admissible, so long as it is made spontaneously and without time for reflection? In England, such an exception to the rule has been recognized and is not limited to a statement made on the first encounter with the police.[17]

For example, in *Tooke*,[18] the accused was charged with unlawful wounding. He had been involved in an altercation in the lavatory of a public house during which he and the victim were injured. The bar manager gave evidence that immediately after the incident, the two men blamed each other. The accused then went voluntarily to the police station and made a statement setting out his version of the events. The bar manager had been permitted to tell the court what the accused had said but the trial judge had refused to allow defense counsel to elicit from the officer what that accused had said at the police station. The English Court of Appeal said that his ruling was correct. The statement to the bar manager was spontaneous and showed the accused's reaction shortly after the incident. Although the statement at the police station was also spontaneous, it would add nothing to his reaction to the suggestion that he had committed the assault. Lord Chief Justice Lane, delivering the judgment of the Court, laid down a threefold test for admissibility — spontaneity, relevance and whether the statement which is sought to be admitted added any weight to the other testimony which had been given in the case.

In Canada, no recognition has been formally given to this specific exception, although such evidence will be admitted where it is considered to be part of the *res gestae*. If and when Canadian courts begin to recognize a separate category of exception, guidelines should be given to assist the trial judge in determining where the dividing line lies. However, so long as the statement is a spontaneous reaction of the accused, there is no reason why it should not to be received, leaving the question of its weight to be determined by the trier of fact.

---

[17] *Pearce* (1979), 69 Cr.App.R. 365.
[18] (1990), 90 Cr.App.R. 417.

5

Character Evidence

1. THE RULE

One of the most important rules of evidence is that the prosecution is generally not allowed to give evidence of an accused's bad character or previous convictions to show that he probably committed the offence charged. One exception to that rule is section 360 of the *Criminal Code*.[1] It contains an unusual provision which allows the Crown, in prosecutions for possession of stolen property or stolen mail, to introduce evidence of an accused's prior convictions for theft or possession within the previous five years for the purpose of proving that he knew that the property was unlawfully obtained.

The general rule excluding character evidence is unique to the common law system of criminal justice. In many countries, evidence of an accused's character is not only admissible, it is the first to be adduced at his trial. Those countries believe that a man's previous history and conduct is relevant to the issue of whether he may be guilty of the charge he is now facing.

There is a great deal of merit in that view. As a matter of common sense, everyone of us takes into account the history and character of someone with whom we are dealing. The common law, however, has historically rejected the view that the disposition of a person is relevant to his guilt. And the common law does not

---

[1] R.S.C. 1985, c. C-46.

purport to be based on common sense, but on a number of policy reasons. The first reason is the one of fairness. It is obviously fairer to compel the prosecution to try a man on the facts of the particular case than on his whole life. The second is that since criminal cases are generally tried by juries, it is important that the jury be allowed to focus on the particular issues to be proved rather than be sidetracked by what the accused may have done on other occasions. There is always the risk that jurors, who have no legal training or experience, may be unduly influenced by the accused's previous conduct. They may conclude that because of his previous criminal habits, he is probably guilty of the offence. As one judge has said,

> The evidence is relevant to the issue, but is excluded for reasons of policy and humanity; because although by admitting it you may arrive at justice in one case out of a hundred, you would probably do injustice in the other ninety-nine.[2]

The general rule was stated by Lord Herschell L.C. in *Makin v. A.G. for New South Wales*,[3]

> It is undoubtedly not competent for the prosecution to adduce evidence tending to show that the accused has been guilty of criminal acts other than those covered by the indictment, for the purpose of leading to the conclusion that the accused is a person likely from his criminal conduct or character to have committed the offence for which he is being tried. On the other hand, the mere fact that the evidence adduced tends to show the commission of other crimes does not render it inadmissible if it be relevant to an issue before the jury, and it may be so relevant if it bears upon the question whether the acts alleged to constitute the crime charged in the indictment were designed or accidental, or to rebut a defence which would otherwise be open to the accused. The statement of these general principles is easy, but it is obvious that it may often be very difficult to draw the line and to decide whether a particular piece of evidence is on one side or the other.

2. EXCEPTIONS TO THE RULE

(a) When The Accused Puts His Character In Issue

Although the rule is that the Crown may not adduce evidence of bad character, that rule applies only to the prosecution. An

---

[2] *Rowton* (1865), L.& C. 520 per Willes J., at p. 541.
[3] (1894) A.C. 57 at p. 65.

accused is always entitled to introduce evidence of his own good character. Indeed, the fact that the accused may have lived a good and honest life to date may be the only defence that he has to the crime charged against him. Evidence of good character may be considered by the trier in determining the credibility of the accused and whether he is the kind of person who would have committed the offence.[4]

Recently, however, the Supreme Court of Canada has said that in cases involving sexual assaults upon young children, evidence of good character will not, as a matter of common sense, have very much weight. The Court noted that since sexual misconduct usually occurs in private, it will not be reflected in the reputation of a person in the community.[5] Nevertheless, even in cases of sexual misconduct involving children, trial judges are required to tell the jury that they must not ignore character evidence altogether; it is simply not entitled to the same weight as it would have with other offences.[6]

An accused may lead evidence of his character in one of two ways. First of all, he may go into the witness stand and swear not only that he did not commit the crime, but that he is not the kind of person who would commit such a crime. However, the mere denial of guilt or repudiation of the allegations against him alone does not amount to placing his character in issue.[7] Secondly, the accused is entitled to call witnesses to attest to his good character. These witnesses are not allowed to give their personal opinion of the accused's good character, nor to point out specific incidents of good character or citizenship, such as the fact that the accused may have saved the life of a child or returned a wallet that he found in the street (although this rule is not always strictly enforced). The rule is that the witness can only swear to the general reputation of the accused in the community and not give his personal opinion of him. The community, however, is not restricted to the community where the accused lives. In *Lavasseur*,[8] the Alberta Court of Appeal said that evidence of the accused's reputation in the

---

[4] *McMillan* (1975), 29 C.R.N.S. 191, 23 C.C.C. (2d) 160 (Ont. C.A.); *Molnar* (1990), 76 C.R. (3d) 125, 55 C.C.C. (3d) 446 (Ont. C.A.).

[5] *Profit* (1994), 24 C.R. (4th) 279, 85 C.C.C. (3d) 232 (S.C.C.).

[6] *Norman* (1994), 26 C.R. (4th) 256, 87 C.C.C. (3d) 153 (Ont. C.A.).

[7] *Shortreed* (1990), 75 C.R. (3d) 306, 54 C.C.C. (3d) 292 (Ont. C.A.).

[8] (1987), 56 C.R. 335 (Alta. C.A.).

business community is admissible because it reflects the modern metropolitan reality, in which frequently not even neighbour's names are known, let alone their general reputation.

Evidence of a person's character is generally handled this way. The witness will be asked whether he or she knows the accused's reputation for honesty in the community (where the crime is one of dishonesty) or peacefulness (where the crime is one of violence), etc. If the witness answers in the affirmative, he or she will then be asked "What is that reputation" and the witness will be allowed to give evidence of the communities' view.

Once the accused calls evidence of his good character, he puts his character in issue. Thus, it is only fair that the prosecution be allowed the right to answer that evidence by calling evidence of the accused's bad character. Evidence of the accused's bad character may be led in the same way, that is, by witnesses who disagree with the witnesses for the accused and who wish to testify as to the accused's bad reputation in the community. Section 666 of the *Code* also gives the Crown the right to call evidence of the accused's bad character by introducing evidence of the accused's previous convictions for offences. Section 667 of the *Code* sets out the method by which such previous convictions may be proved. If the accused gives evidence in his defence, he may also be cross-examined with respect to his previous character or his previous convictions (a matter which will be dealt with in section (c) post).

(b) Where The Accused Puts The Victim's Character In Issue

The general rule is that a victim's character is not admissible on the issue of whether the accused committed the offence. Even bad people are entitled to protection from having crimes committed against them. However, there may be instances where the character of the victim is relevant to the defence of the accused. For example, if the accused is charged with a crime of violence such as murder, manslaughter or assault, and claims self-defence, the victim's disposition for violence may be relevant as to who was the aggressor.[9] Similarly, if the defence says that it was not the accused who committed the offence but a third party, evidence of the third

---

[9] *Scopelliti* (1981), 63 C.C.C. (2d) 481 (Ont. C.A.).

party's character for violence would have probative value provided that the third party had the propensity to commit the type of act in question and was connected with the circumstances surrounding the charge.[10] Evidence of a third party's character or violent disposition has been held to be admissible even if it refers only to one event.[11]

Evidence of the deceased's disposition for violence under the *Scopelliti* rule is not restricted only to those instances where the accused claimed that he acted in self-defence. It may in some instances be lead where the defence is accident. For example, in *Sims*,[12] the defence was that the deceased was killed when he lunged at the accused with a knife during an altercation and in the struggle by the accused to prevent the deceased from using it, he was accidently stabbed. It was held that evidence of the deceased's disposition for violence was admissible because, if accepted by the jury, it tended to support the accused's evidence that it was the deceased who produced the knife and attacked him.

Evidence of the victim's disposition for violence may be brought out through the cross-examination of Crown witnesses or by the defence calling evidence of the victim's general reputation in the community for violence. In such instance, it is only fair that the prosecution be allowed, by way of reply, to establish that the accused also has a propensity for violence and that it was he, not the victim, who was the aggressor.

In England, the accused is protected from questions about his previous criminal convictions or questions tending to show previous bad character unless he puts his own character in issue or attacks the character of the Crown witnesses. The English rule is essentially a tit-for-tat rule. So long as the defence does not attack the prosecution, the prosecution is not entitled to attack the defence. This rule is contained in the *Criminal Evidence Act* of 1898.

Canada has no similar provision. The suggestion by the defence that a Crown witness may not be telling the truth does not give the prosecution, under Canadian law, the right to attack the accused by leading evidence of his bad character. As already indicated, the only recognized exception arises where the defence is one of self-

---

[10] *Arcangioli* (1994), 27 C.R. (4th) 1, 87 C.C.C. (3d) 289 (S.C.C.).
[11] *Yaeck* (1991), 10 C.R. (4th) 1, 68 C.C.C. (3d) 545 (Ont C.A.), at p. 563 (C.C.C.).
[12] (1994), 28 C.R. (4th) 231, 87 C.C.C. (3d) 402 (B.C. C.A.).

defence and possibly accident.[13] Here the Crown is only allowed to call evidence of the accused's disposition for violence in reply to the defence's suggestion that it was the victim who was the aggressor.

(c) When The Accused Testifies

At common law, an accused was not allowed to give evidence in his own defence. This rule was based on the civil practice which prohibited persons from testifying in a case which affected their interest. In Canada, the right of an accused to testify on his own behalf was first recognized in 1886 with respect to some offences, and later in 1893 by the *Canada Evidence Act*[14] with respect to all offences. Section 4(1) of the *Act* provides that,

> 4(1) Every person charged with an offence, and, except as otherwise provided in this section, the wife or husband, as the case may be, of the person so charged, is a competent witness for the defence whether the person so charged is charged solely or jointly with any other person.

This means that although an accused has the right to give evidence on his own behalf, he cannot be forced to go into the witness box if he does not wish to do so.

An accused who chooses to testify on his own behalf is in the same position as any other witness. When he does, he puts himself forward as a credible person. His credibility becomes relevant to the truth and accuracy of his testimony. Thus, his credibility is subject to attack by cross-examination as any other witness would be. However, it has been recognized that the right of the Crown to attack the credibility of an accused is not superior to the policy rule which protects an accused against an attack upon his character. While an accused, like any ordinary witness, is generally open to cross-examination at large as to credibility, he may not be cross-examined by the prosecution as to previous misconduct or discreditable associations for the purpose of attacking his credibility, unless such cross-examination is relevant to prove the falsity of his own evidence.[15] That protection, however, does not extend to the case of an accused

---

[13] *Sims, supra*, note 12.
[14] R.S.C. 1985, c. C-5.
[15] *Davison* (1974), 20 C.C.C. (2d) 424 (Ont. C.A.).

who cross-examines a co-accused who has given damning evidence against him. In such instance, it is open for the accused to ask the co-accused questions about his character to show that he is a disreputable person not worthy of belief.[16] The policy of the law is that the right of an accused to full answer and defence does not allow him to hide under that umbrella of protection thereby impairing the right of his co-accused to full answer and defence by asking questions pertinent to his defence.

The criminal record of a witness or the accused stands on a different level. Section 12(1) of the *Act* provides,

> 12(1) A witness may be questioned as to whether he has been convicted of any offence, and on being so questioned, if he either denies the fact or refuses to answer, the opposite party may prove the conviction.

In England, section 1(f) of the *Act*, 1898 forbids cross-examination of an accused on his record unless: it is relevant to a fact in issue; the accused leads evidence of his own good character; the accused impugns the character of the prosecutor or his witness; or gives evidence against a co-accused. In Canada, there is no such protection. Section 12(1) of the *Act* permits the Crown to cross-examine an accused about his criminal record even if he does not attack the Crown witnesses or lead evidence of his own good character.

For a long time, it was believed that a trial judge had a general discretion to exclude evidence of an accused's prior convictions where the revelation of those convictions would prejudice him in the eyes of the jury.[17] However, four years before the enactment of the *Charter of Rights and Freedoms*,[18] it was decided that a trial judge had no discretion to prevent the Crown from cross-examining the accused as to prior convictions for any offence.[19] Moreover, it was held that the word "any offence" in section 12(1) included convictions for offences committed outside of Canada provided that the process of adjudication of guilt constituted a conviction under Canadian law. In an earlier case, it was also decided that a

---

[16] *Jackson* (1992), 9 C.R. (4th) 57, 68 C.C.C. (3d) 385 (Ont. C.A.).

[17] *Powell* (1977), 37 C.C.C. (2d) 117 (Ont. Cty. Ct); *Skehan* (1978), 39 C.C.C. (2d) 196 (Ont. H.C.).

[18] *Canadian Charter of Rights and Freedoms*, Part 1 of the Constitution Act, 1982, being Schedule B to the Canada Act 1982 (U.K.), 1982, c. 11.

[19] *Stratton* (1978), 3 C.R. (3d) 289, 42 C.C.C. (2d) 449 (Ont. C.A.).

"conviction" included the sentence so that the accused could be cross-examined on the penalty imposed.[20]

However in 1988, the Supreme Court of Canada decided that section 12(1) was not so absolute in its terms. In *Corbett*,[21] the Court ruled that a trial judge did have a discretion to exclude evidence of previous convictions in those cases where a mechanical application of section 12 would undermine the right to a fair trial as guaranteed by the *Charter*. The Court recognized that although it was impossible to provide an exhaustive catalogue of the factors that are relevant in assessing the probative value or prejudice of such evidence, some of those factors were the nature of the prior conviction, its similarity to the conduct for which the accused is on trial and the remoteness or nearness of the prior conviction.

The Court noted that if the purpose of permitting cross-examination on a prior conviction is to test credibility, then a conviction which involves an act of deceit, fraud, cheating or stealing is more probative of a person's credibility than an act of violence which had little or no direct bearing on a person's veracity or integrity. The Court also noted that the similarity of the prior conviction to the charge before the court created a potential for prejudice unless the evidence met the stringent test for admitting similar fact evidence.[22] Finally, it was held that a conviction which occurred long before, even one which involved an act of dishonesty, should be generally excluded on the ground of remoteness.

As noted previously, section 1(f) of the English *Criminal Evidence Act*,[23] 1898 forbids cross-examination of an accused on his record unless it is relevant to a fact in issue, the accused leads evidence of his own good character, impugns the character of the prosecutor or his witness, or gives evidence against a co-accused. In *Corbett*,[23] Mr. Justice LaForest recognized that Canada had no such rule and was concerned about fairness to the Crown of prohibiting the cross-examination of the accused on prior convictions where the defence has made a deliberate attack upon the credibility of a Crown witness, particularly where the case boils down to a credibility contest between the accused and that witness. Although he

---

[20] *Boyce* (1974), 28 C.R.N.S. 336, 23 C.C.C. (2d) 16 (Ont. C.A.).

[21] (1988), 64 C.R. (3d) 1, 41 C.C.C. (3d) 385 (S.C.C.).

[22] *P. (G.F.)* (1994), 29 C.R. (4th) 315, 89 C.C.C. (3d) 176 (Ont. C.A.); *Trudel* (1994), 90 C.C.C. (3d) 318 (Que. C.A.).

[23] *Supra*, note 21.

was prepared to recognize that in such instance, the jury was entitled to have before it the record of the person attacking the character of the Crown witness in order to determine whether he was any more worthy of belief than the person attacked, he felt that this was not a factor that should override the concern for a fair trial.

(d) When The Evidence Is Of Similar Facts

At the outset of this chapter, it was pointed out that although as a matter of common sense, the disposition of a person may point to his guilt or innocence, such evidence is excluded because the law considers it unfair to allow the prosecution to try a man on his whole life rather than on the facts of the case. Another reason is to ensure that the jury's attention is not diverted from the central issue in the case. On the other hand, there may be instances where evidence of a person's bad character or disposition is so probative of the particular issues in the case that it should be admitted. As Lord Hershell L.C. pointed out in the second part of his classic statement of the rule in *Makin v. A.G. for New South Wales*[24]

> On the other hand, the mere fact that the evidence adduced tends to show the commission of other crimes does not render it inadmissible if it be relevant to an issue before the jury, and it *may be so relevant if it bears upon the question whether the acts alleged to constitute the crime charged in the indictment were designed or accidental, or to rebut a defence which would otherwise be open to the accused.* The statement of these general principles is easy, but it is obvious that it may often be very difficult to draw the line and to decide whether a particular piece of evidence is on the one side or the other. [Emphasis added][25]

In the years that followed Lord Hershell's judgment, judges, lawyers and legal scholars attempted "to draw the line" in an effort to make some sense of the rule. Judges approached their task by creating categories of relevance in an effort to place each case in a particular pigeon hole. Evidence was admitted if the prosecution was able to show that the evidence went "to prove intent" or "to prove a system" or "to prove a plan" or "to show malice" or "to rebut the defence of accident or mistake" or "to prove identity" or "to rebut the defence of innocent association." However, in 1975,

---

[24] *Supra*, note 3.
[25] *Supra*, note 3 at p. 65.

the House of Lords in *Boardman v. D.P.P.*[26] decided that although the categories were useful illustrations of the similar fact rule, they were no longer an automatic ticket to admissibility. The House said that the proper approach to be followed in the future was for the trial judge to balance the probative value of the evidence against the prejudice which the accused might suffer if the evidence was admitted. In one of the speeches, Lord Wilberforce said,

> The basic principle must be that the admission of similar fact evidence... is exceptional and requires a strong degree of probative force. This probative force is derived, if at all, from the circumstances that the facts testified to by the several witness bear to each other such a striking similarity that they must, when judged by experience and common sense, either all be true, or have arisen from a common cause to the witnesses or from pure coincidence. The jury may, therefore, properly be asked to judge whether the right conclusion is that all are true, so that each story is supported by the other.[27]

The *Boardman* approach was adopted three years later by the Supreme Court of Canada in *Guay*[28] and reaffirmed by the Court in *Sweitzer*.[29] In *B.(C.R.)*,[30] Madame Justice McLachlin, writing for the majority, added,

> The judge must consider such factors as the degree of distinctiveness or uniqueness between the similar fact evidence and the offences alleged against the accused, as well as the connection, if any, of the evidence *to issues other than propensity*, to the end of determining whether, in the context of the case before him, the probative value of the evidence outweighs its potential prejudice and justifies its reception.

Before the trial judge can begin to weigh the probative value of the evidence versus its potential prejudice, he must first identify the fact in issue which the evidence is adduced to prove. In Chapter 1, it was pointed out that in every criminal trial, there are three factual issues which the Crown must prove to establish a successful prosecution: the act, that is that a crime was committed; the identity of the perpetrator; and the intent of the perpetrator. Whenever the Crown seeks to have similar fact evidence admitted, the judge should be told by the prosecution of the issue or issues towards

---

[26] (1975), 60 Cr. App. R. 165.
[27] *Ibid.*, at pp. 174-175.
[28] (1978), 6 C.R. (3d) 130, 42 C.C.C. (2d) 536 (S.C.C.).
[29] (1982), 29 C.R. (3d) 97, 68 C.C.C. (2d) 193 (S.C.C.).
[30] (1990), 76 C.R. (3d) 1, 55 C.C.C. (3d) 1 (S.C.C.).

which the evidence is directed. In some instances, the similar fact evidence will be relevant to a single issue; in other, it may be relevant to all three issues.

The *Makin*[31] case is a good example of where the similar fact evidence was adduced to prove all three issues. Makin and his wife were charged with the murder of a child whose body had been found in their back garden. The Makins had agreed to look after the child and had received a very small amount of money from the child's mother. The bodies of eleven other infants who had been entrusted to their care for a very small amount of money were also found buried in the gardens of houses occupied by the Makins at various times. Although no one had seen the Makins kill any of the children, it was held that such evidence was admissible to show that the children had died, not from natural causes or by accident, but by design. The evidence was tendered to show that the only natural or irresistible inference that the jury could draw was that the child had died by design (the act) and that it was the Makins who had killed him (identity) and that they intended to do so (intent).

The issues may or may not become more difficult where the defence admits one or more issues, leaving a single issue in dispute. In the famous "Brides in the Bath" case,[32] the issue was whether a crime had been committed at all. Smith had married successively three women all of whom had drowned, supposedly accidentally, in a bath that he had arranged to have installed. In each case, Smith benefited financially from their deaths. He was charged with the murder of his first wife and the prosecution was granted the right to call evidence as to the circumstances surrounding the deaths of his second and third wives. The English Court of Criminal Appeal held that the evidence was admissible to rebut the defence of accident, that is whether it was a crime at all. Although there was no evidence directly connecting Smith with the death of any of his wives, the court held that it was highly unlikely that all three could have died by accident.

The trial judge, Scrutton J., charged the jury this way,

> If you find an accident which benefits a person and you find that the person has been sufficiently fortunate to have that accident happen to him a number of times, benefiting him each time, you draw a very strong, frequently

---

[31] *Supra*, note 3.
[32] *Smith* (1915), 11 Cr. App. R. 229.

and irresistible inference, that the occurrence of so many accidents benefiting him is such a coincidence that it can not have happened unless it was designed.[33]

Although *Makin*[34] and *Smith*[35] are often regarded as straightforward examples of the application of the similar fact evidence exception, it is significant to note that in both cases the similar acts were not evidence of criminal acts on their face. They only became evidence of crimes when the jury inferred, because of the similarity and number of incidents, that the death of the victims was as a result of the deliberate act of the accused.

A question that has constantly vexed the courts is the degree of distinctiveness that the evidence must bear to be regarded as a similar fact? In *Boardman*,[36] the House of Lords suggested that similar fact evidence might be introduced where it was strikingly similar, or had common unusual and highly distinctive features. An example given in *Boardman* was the *Straffen* case.[37] Straffen was accused of the murder of a little girl who was found strangled. No attempt had been made to assault her sexually or to conceal her body, although it might easily have been done. Straffen, who had just escaped from Broadmoor and was in the neighbourhood at the time of the crime, had previously committed two murders of young girls. These murders had the same peculiar features. It was held that it would have been a most extraordinary coincidence if, while Straffen was temporarily at large, another madman in the same area had killed the little girl by strangulation, and had neither assaulted her nor made any attempt to conceal her.

Although in some instances, such as the *Straffen* case, the distinctive features between the similar fact evidence and the offence charged will support the conclusion that the accused committed the offence, it is usually necessary for the Crown to lead evidence connecting the accused with the crime charged before similar fact evidence will be admitted. For example, in *Sweitzer*,[38] the accused was originally charged with fifteen counts of sexual assault on women but, before the trial began, the trial judge severed the various counts.

---

[33] *Supra*, note 32.
[34] *Supra*, note 3.
[35] *Supra*, note 32.
[36] *Supra*, note 26.
[37] (1952), 36 Cr. App. R. 132 (C.A.).
[38] *Supra*, note 29.

The prosecution then elected to proceed on the first count and was permitted by the judge to lead evidence of the other fourteen assaults as similar fact evidence. Although there was some direct evidence identifying Sweitzer as the assailant in four of those assault, the victims were unable to identify their assailant in the other eleven. Although there was some similarity between the conduct of the assailant in those four episodes with the conduct of the assailant in the eleven episodes where he could not be identified, Mr. Justice McIntyre of the Supreme Court of Canada held that the trial judge had erred in admitting evidence of the eleven episodes because they were not shown to be connected in any way with Sweitzer.

In an effort to describe the high degree of probative force that must exist before similar fact evidence will be admissible, the judges in *Boardman*[39] came up with the catch-phrase "strikingly similar". However, the Ontario Court of Appeal, in two cases that were decided after *Boardman*, said that it was not necessary that the evidence be "strikingly similar". In the first, *McNamara (No. 1)*,[40] the Court said that evidence of striking similarity was not necessary where the evidence is tendered to prove a state of mind, knowledge, intent, authority or system. In the second, *Carpenter (No. 2)*,[41] an arson case, the Court said that evidence of striking similarity with respect to fires was not required where the defence raised was that of accident. Carpenter was the owner of property destroyed in a fire and the beneficiary of a fire insurance policy on the property. There was evidence that he had been on the premises a few hours before the fire occurred. The trial judge had excluded evidence of two other fires within a six month period at the premises because the evidence as to those fires was not strikingly similar.

However, the requirement for similar fact evidence to be strikingly similar was re-affirmed by the Supreme Court of Canada in *C.(M.H.)*.[42] There Madame Justice McLachlin wrote,

> That probative value usually arises from the fact that the acts compared are so strikingly similar that their similarities cannot be attributed to coincidence.

---

[39] *Supra*, note 26.
[40] (1981), 56 C.C.C. (2d) 193 (Ont. C.A.).
[41] (1982), 1 C.C.C. (3d) 149 (Ont. C.A.).
[42] (1991), 4 C.R. (4th) 1, 63 C.C.C. (3d) 385 (S.C.C.).

Ironically, a requirement of striking similarity was subsequently rejected by the House of Lords in *D.P.P. v. P.*[43] There, Lord McKay of Clashfern L.C., after reviewing *Boardman*, concluded that all that the judges were saying in that case was that "striking similarity" was only one way of showing that the similar fact sought to be admitted possessed the necessary high degree of probative force. The degree of similarity required before such evidence would be admitted was never constant but varied with the nature of the similar fact evidence and the issue which it was lead to prove.

> This relationship, from which support is derived, may take many forms and while these forms may include "striking similarity" in the manner in which the crime is committed, consisting of unusual characteristics in its execution the necessary relationship is by no means confined to such circumstances. Relationships in time and circumstances other than these may well be important relationships in this connection. Where the identity of the perpetrator is in issue, and evidence of this kind is important in that connection, obviously something in the nature of what has been called in the course of argument a signature or other special feature will be necessary. To transpose this requirement to other situations where the question is whether a crime has been committed, rather than who did commit it, is to impose an unnecessary and improper restriction upon the application of the principle.[44]

One area that has caused difficulty is where the accused is a member of an abnormal group with the same propensities as the perpetrator of a crime. At one time, there was authority that evidence of a man's homosexuality was admissible on a charge of indecent assault to rebut the defence of innocent association,[45] or to prove identity.[46] That view was rejected in *Boardman* and again by the Supreme Court of Canada in *Morin*.[47] In *Morin*, Mr. Justice Sopinka said that there also had to be some further distinguishing feature.

> Accordingly, if the crime was committed by someone with homosexual tendencies, it is not sufficient to establish that the accused is a practising homosexual, or indeed is engaged in numerous homosexual acts. The tendered evidence must tend to show that there was some striking similarity between

---

[43] (1991), 93 Cr.App.R. 267.
[44] *Supra*, note 43 at p. 280.
[45] *King* (1966), 51 Cr.App.R. 46.
[46] *Glynn* (1971), 15 C.R.N.S. 343, 5 C.C.C. (2d) 364 (Ont. C.A.).
[47] (1988), 66 C.R. (3d) 1, 44 C.C.C. (3d) 193 (S.C.C.).

the manner in which the perpetrator committed the criminal act and such evidence.[48]

One problem that has received scant attention is the degree of proof that must be established before the trier can consider the similar fact evidence in relation to the offence before the court. The weight of authority suggests that the onus is not proof beyond a reasonable doubt but something akin to the civil onus. Juries are generally told that they can use similar fact evidence to assist them in deciding whether the accused committed the offence charged "if they believe it".[49]

That view, however, is difficult to reconcile with the rule that if an accused has been acquitted of a previous incident, evidence of that previous incident may not be used as similar fact evidence against him.[50] Indeed, the Ontario Court of Appeal has gone further and held that if the trial judge admits evidence of similar acts that are later prosecuted resulting in an acquittal, then any conviction based on evidence of those similar acts must result in a new trial.[51]

In *G.(K.R.)*,[52] at the accused's trial on charges of sexual assault, the Crown was allowed to introduce as similar fact evidence the testimony of a child who was also allegedly sexually assaulted by the accused. The accused was convicted. He was then tried on a charge of sexually assaulting the child based on the evidence that had been introduced as similar fact evidence and acquitted of this charge. On the appeal of his conviction, the accused applied to introduce as fresh evidence the fact of his acquittal and his application was granted. It was held that if the accused had been tried and acquitted of the charge of sexual assault upon the child before the trial which gave rise to the appeal, that child's evidence would not have been admissible as similar fact evidence.[53] The court also noted the well established principle of the criminal law that an acquit-

---

[48] *Ibid.*
[49] *Simpson* (1977), 35 C.C.C. (2d) 337 (Ont. C.A.); *Lawson* (1971), 14 C.R.N.S. 377, 3 C.C.C. 372 (Alta C.A.).
[50] *Cullen* (1990), 52 C.C.C. (3d) 459 (Ont. C.A.); *Grdic* (1985), 19 C.C.C. (3d) 289 (S.C.C.).
[51] *G. (K.R.)* (1992), 68 C.C.C. (3d) 268 (Ont. C.A.).
[52] *Supra*, note 51.
[53] *Cullen, supra*, note 50.

tal is the equivalent of a finding of innocence.[54] Therefore, it had to be assumed that the accused was innocent of the allegations made against him by the child.

---

[54] *Grant* (1991), 7 C.R. (4th) 388, 67 C.C.C. (3d) 268 (S.C.C.).

6

Opinion Evidence

1. THE RULE

A witness is not allowed to express his personal belief or give his opinion about a fact in issue unless the matter calls for his special skill or knowledge, and he is an expert in such matters. This rule is based upon the notion that it is possible to draw a distinction between a fact and the inference to be drawn from that fact. Witnesses are supposed to testify as to matters which they observe through their senses, that is eyes, ears, nose, etc. It is for the jury to decide what is the proper inference to be drawn from the facts established by the witness.

The difficulty with the rule is that it is not always easy to draw a line between fact and opinion. For example, when a witness says that "the car was going very fast" or that "the accused was angry" or that "the girl was very pretty" or "the person is very old", the witness is really expressing his personal opinion based on his own experience and view of matters. Yet, such evidence is routinely given in court without objection. Indeed, in an Ontario case, *German*,[1] a witness was allowed to give evidence that the accused was intoxicated. Chief Justice Robertson justified the reception of that evidence in this way,

> No doubt, the general rule is that it is only persons who are qualified by some special skill, training or experience who can be asked their opinion upon a matter in issue. The rule is not, however, an absolute one. There are a number of

---

[1] (1947), 3 C.R. 516, [1947] O.R. 395 (Ont. C.A.).

matters in respect of which a person of ordinary intelligence may be permitted to give evidence of his opinion upon a matter of which he has personal knowledge. Such matters as the identity of individuals, the apparent age of a person, the speed of a vehicle, are among the matters upon which witnesses have been allowed to express an opinion, notwithstanding that they have no special qualifications, other than the fact they have personal knowledge of the subject matter, to enable them to form an opinion.

Not all courts, however, have adopted this liberal approach to the general rule. For example in *Browne*,[2] the question was whether a witness could identify a person as the perpetrator of a crime. O'Halloran J.A. argued,

> A positive statement 'that is the man', when rationalized, is found to be an opinion and not a statement of single fact. All a witness can say is, that because of this or that he remembers about a person, he is of opinion that person is 'the man'. A witness recognizes a person because of a certain personality that person has acquired in the eyes of the witness. That personality is reflected by characteristics of the person, which, when associated with something in the mind of the witness, causes the latter to remember that person in a way the witness does not remember any other person.

> Unless the witness is able to testify with confidence what characteristics and what 'something' has stirred and clarified his memory or recognition, then an identification confined to 'that is the man', standing by itself, cannot be more than a vague general description and is untrustworthy in any sphere of life where certitude is essential.

Nevertheless, the courts have continued to allow an ordinary witness to give evidence on a "subject about which most people should be able to express an opinion from their ordinary day-to-day experience of life." These include such matters as disputed handwriting if the witness has acquired previous knowledge of the handwriting of a person whose handwriting is in dispute,[3] the age of another person, his own mental or physical condition, whether a person is intoxicated or impaired by alcohol, the degree of intoxication, and whether the person's ability to drive is impaired;[4] and estimates of such things as speed, distance, size, etc.

---

[2] (1951), 99 C.C.C. 141 (B.C. C.A.).
[3] *Derrick* (1910), 5 Cr. App. R. 162.
[4] *Graat* (1983), 31 C.R. (3d) 289, 2 C.C.C. (3d) 365 (S.C.C.).

2. EXPERT OPINION

An exception to the rule exists in favour of witnesses who are classified as experts. The theory underlying expert testimony is that experts, because of their knowledge, training and experience are able to form better opinions on a given state of facts than opinions formed by those not so well equipped such as ordinary jurors. Their opinions are admitted in evidence to aid the jury to understand questions which inexperienced persons are not likely to decide correctly without such assistance. However, if the subject is one of common knowledge and the facts can be intelligibly described to the jury, and they can form a reasonable opinion for themselves, the opinion of an expert will be rejected.

An expert is therefore someone who is qualified by study or experience to form a definite opinion of his own respecting a division of science, branch of art or department of trade, which persons having no particular training or special study are incapable of accurately forming. It is not a university degree that makes a person an expert; it is his special knowledge by study or practical experience.

On the other hand, the fact that a witness may have knowledge about a subject or understand it better than the judge or jury does not necessarily justify receiving his evidence. If the judge or jury can become sufficiently informed about the subject during the trial so that they can reach an accurate conclusion, there is really no basis for the expert opinion.

Thus, the admissibility of expert evidence will depend upon four criteria: relevance; necessity in assisting the trier of fact; absence of any exclusionary rule; and a properly qualified expert.[5] In determining relevance, the trial judge must consider whether the probative value of the evidence is overborne by its prejudicial effect and whether it can influence the trier of fact out of proportion to its reliability.[6] If there is the danger that the expert evidence would be misused, distort the fact finding process or confuse the jury, then the trial judge should not admit it. Moreover, the trial judge has the duty to subject a novel scientific theory or technique to special scrutiny to ensure that it meets the four criteria.

---

[5] *Mohan* (1994), 29 C.R. (4th) 243, 89 C.C.C. (3d) 402 (S.C.C.), reversing (1992), 13 C.R. (4th) 292, 71 C.C.C. (3d) 1321 (Ont. C.A.).
[6] *Melaragni* (1992), 73 C.C.C. (3d) 348 (Ont. Gen. Div.).

Before a witness is permitted to give expert evidence, he must first be properly qualified as an expert by the side that calls him; he must also be accepted by the court as an expert on the particular area of expertise about which he is to testify. Although the other side will often admit the witness's qualifications, there is still an obligation upon the trial judge to be satisfied that the expert's testimony meets the four criteria.

Once qualified and accepted by the court to give expert testimony, the witness may be permitted to express his opinion on the conclusion which should be drawn from certain facts. He may have personal knowledge of the facts; but more often than not, he will have to rely on information given to him by others. In this later instance, he will be asked to give his opinion on what is called a hypothesis or a hypothetical question. He will be asked to assume certain facts which will be outlined to him. He will then be asked for his opinion on the conclusion that should be drawn from those facts. However, the opinion expressed must only relate to the facts; the expert is not entitled to give an answer that involves a conclusion of law.

If the opinion of an expert is premised upon the truth of facts which the expert assumes hypothetically, those assumed facts must be established by evidence in the usual way, otherwise the basis of the expert's opinion collapses. Indeed, the judge must warn the jury or instruct himself that before the opinion can be considered, they must be satisfied as to the truth of the facts upon which the expert is relying. Thus an attack on the facts assumed by the expert is usually one of the ways a cross-examiner will attempt to discredit the expert's opinion.

It is a common practice in those instances where a psychiatrist is called upon to give an opinion as to the mental state of the accused to rely upon interviews with the accused and with others, all of which form part of the accused's psychiatric history. It is important to remember that in such instance, what is being relied upon by the court is the expert opinion of the psychiatrist, not the statements made by the accused and others. Although there is a common complaint that the expert's opinion is dependant upon the truth of the statements relied upon by the expert, this will not affect the admissibility of the opinion although it is a factor in assessing the weight of it.[7] At the same time, however, the trial judge must be careful to warn the jury that in considering the weight of the opinion, they must be satisfied of the truth of the statements relied upon by the psychiatrist.

On the other hand, if the psychiatrist (or any other expert) is present during the course of the trial and is asked at the conclusion to give his opinion based on the evidence he has heard, such evidence is not admissible. The reason is that what the expert is being asked to do is to pass on the truthfulness of the witnesses who have testified and that is within the exclusive jurisdiction of the trier of fact.[8]

Another common complaint about expert evidence is that the expert may be giving his opinion on the very issue which the judge and jury must decide and thus usurp their function. Whether the evidence is simply opinion to assist the trier in deciding the ultimate issue or evidence of the very issue is not often easy to determine. For example, if the issue is whether the accused was criminally responsible for an act committed while suffering from a mental disorder, a psychiatrist called as an expert will be asked to give his opinion about whether the accused was capable of "appreciating the nature and quality of his acts" or "of knowing that his acts were wrong" in accordance with section 16 of the *Criminal Code*.[9] Such evidence is regularly received even though it would appear to be on the very issue which the judge or jury must decide.

The courts have always had difficulty with the application of the ultimate issue rule. For example, in *Lupien*,[10] the accused was charged with gross indecency. His defence was that he thought that the male person with whom he was found was, in fact, a female, and attempted to introduce psychiatric evidence to show that he had a strong aversion to homosexual practices and therefore would not knowingly engage in homosexual acts. The Supreme Court of Canada was divided on the issue.

The dissenting judges felt that the psychiatric opinion ought not to be admitted because it came too close to the very question that the jury had to decide on the whole of the evidence. The majority view, however, was that the expert testimony was admis-

---

[7] *Swietlinski* (1978), 5 C.R. (3d) 324, 44 C.C.C. (2d) 267 (Ont. C.A.), at p. 301 (C.C.C.).
[8] *Bleta* (1965), 44 C.R. 193, [1965] 1 C.C.C. 1 (S.C.C.).
[9] R.S.C. 1985, c. C-46.
[10] (1970), 9 C.R.N.S. 165, [1970] 2 C.C.C. 193 (S.C.C.).

sible on the question of whether or not the man was "homosexually inclined or otherwise sexually perverted." Mr. Justice Hall gave these reasons,

> That type of evidence is very close, if not identical, to the conclusion the jury must come to in such a case if it is to find that the accused was not guilty because he did not have intent necessary to support conviction. The weight to be given the opinion of the expert is entirely for the jury, and it is the function of the trial judge to instruct the jury that the responsibility for weighing the evidence is theirs and theirs alone.[11]

The real difficulty facing the jury is when there are two experts expressing diametrically opposed views. This means that their decision will turn not so much on which facts are proved in evidence, but on which expert the jury believes. The result is that their decision will often depend on which expert is more credible than on whose opinion is the correct one. In criminal cases, however, the difficulty for the trier may be more apparent than real. The rule is that before the judge and jury are entitled to accept the opinion of the prosecution expert over the defence expert, they must be satisfied that it is the correct one.[12]

3. OPINION AS TO THE CREDIBILITY OF A WITNESS

One of the most difficult issues facing a trier is determining who is telling the truth, particularly where the central issue at trial is whether a certain event occurred (such as a sexual assault) and there are only two persons present at the event, the complainant and the accused. Should a witness be allowed to give evidence that one of the witnesses to the event is or is not a credible witness? Historically, opinion evidence as to the credibility of a witness has not been allowed, although evidence in the form of character evidence of the witness's reputation in the community for lack of credibility has always been allowed. The reason why opinion evidence has not been allowed is because of the reluctance of allowing evidence on the very issue which the trier must decide. Another concern is that it might prolong the trial unduly by creating confusion and a multiplicity of issues.

---

[11] *Supra*, note 10 at pp. 279-280 (C.C.C.).
[12] *Molnar* (1990), 76 C.R. (3d) 125, 55 C.C.C. (3d) 446 (Ont. C.A.).

However, in *Gunewardene*,[13] the English Court of Criminal Appeal indicated that it was prepared to accept that an impeaching witness was no longer confined to expressing an opinion as to the lack of veracity of a prosecution witness based upon that witness's general reputation. The impeaching witness was entitled to state that from his knowledge of the witness, that witness was unworthy of credit. But the Court would not let the impeaching witness detail his reasons for that opinion even though he was a medical witness. However, thirteen years later, in *Toohey v. Metropolitan Police Commissioner*,[14] the House of Lords overruled *Gunewardene* on that point and said that a medical witness could give his reasons why the witness should not be believed. In Canada, that view was accepted by the Ontario Court of Appeal in *Gonzague*.[15]

In 1986, the Ontario Court of Appeal went further and removed the restrictions upon a lay person giving his reasons why a witness should not be believed. In *T.(S.)*,[16] it was held that the opinions of the defence witnesses that the complainants at a sexual trial ought not to be believed and the basis of their belief were receivable. The Court also said that reply evidence was admissible to reduce the impact of that impeaching evidence. But it was stressed that the jury should also be told that the reply evidence must not be used to bolster the credibility of the complainants.

Although opinion evidence *discrediting* a witness's testimony is receivable, the authorities are clear that evidence *bolstering* a witness's testimony is generally not receivable, even if it is expert testimony. For example, in *Kyselka*,[17] the Crown had called a psychiatrist who had testified that the complainant, a retarded girl who had alleged that she had been raped, was likely, because of her condition, to be a truthful witness. The Ontario Court of Appeal, however, held that evidence bolstering the testimony of a witness was not admissible because it amounted to "oath helping".[18]

Notwithstanding, these clear statements of the law, the courts have in recent years come under increasing pressure to admit medical evidence of the credibility of a complainant in sexual assault

---

[13] (1951), 35 Cr. App. R. 80.
[14] (1964), 49 Cr. App. R. 148.
[15] (1983), 34 C.R. (3d) 169, 4 C.C.C. (3d) 505 (Ont. C.A.).
[16] (1987), 55 C.R. (3d) 321, 31 C.C.C. (3d) 1 (Ont. C.A.).
[17] (1962), 37 C.R. 391, 133 C.C.C. 103 (Ont. C.A.).
[18] *Burkart* (1965), 45 C.R. 383 (Sask. C.A.).

cases. That pressure has been strong, particularly where the complainant is a child or is mentally infirm, because of the ease with which their evidence can be attacked by the defence and the fear that such victims are not receiving the kind of protection from the courts that they need and deserve. In *Beliveau*,[19] Mr. Justice Mac-Farlane was able to sidesstep the general rule this way. He was prepared to admit the testimony of a pediatrician that the complainant, because of her age, was unlikely to have a motive to lie since,

> these question were necessary in assessing the validity of his opinion on an issue in the case, and not to establish that the child was a truthful witness.

In *B.(G.)*[20] the Supreme Court of Canada was prepared to go further. There, three young offenders were charged with the sexual assault of a seven year old child. A psychologist specializing in the treatment of victims of sexual abuse had testified that the changes noted in the victim's behaviour, such as bed-wetting and nightmares, were characteristic of behaviour noted in victims of this type of sexual abuse. It was held that evidence of an expert as to the psychological and physical conditions which frequently arise as a result of sexual abuse of a child was admissible because it provided assistance to the trier of fact in concluding whether an assault had occurred. Since the defence was that there had been no assault, the admissibility of that evidence inferentially bolstered the complainant's credibility on that issue. Nevertheless, Madame Justice Wilson who delivered the judgment of the Court warned that,

> ...the expert evidence should not be used to bolster the credibility of witnesses or indicate that they should be believed since credibility is a matter exclusively reserved for the trier of fact.[21]

In *R.(S.)*,[22] the Ontario Court of Appeal relied on this passage to order a new trial where evidence was called by the Crown to explain why there was a delay of several months between the time that the complainant (a child) first complained of sexual abuse and the date when the charges were laid. The explanation was that a

---

[19] (1986), 30 C.C.C. (3d) 193 (B.C. C.A.).
[20] (1990), 77 C.R. (3d) 327, 56 C.C.C. (3d) 200 (S.C.C.).
[21] *Ibid.*, at 207 (C.C.C.).
[22] (1992), 15 C.R. (4th) 102, 73 C.C.C. (3d) 225 (Ont. C.A.)

social worker believed her but the investigating officer did not. To resolve the issue, a psychologist was called in to conduct an assessment of the child's credibility and the charges were laid. Both the social worker and the psychologist were allowed to give evidence that they believed her before the child testified.

In allowing the appeal, it was held by the Court that the effective purpose of the evidence was to bolster the credibility of the complainant and it was therefore not admissible. It was pointed out that the better way to deal with the question of delay between the report and the charges was to simply the tell the jury that they should not speculate about the delay because it was not a matter that concerned them.

Recently, in *Marquard*[23] the Supreme Court of Canada reaffirmed the general rule that the ultimate conclusion as to the credibility or truthfulness of a particular witness is for the trier of fact, and is not the proper subject of expert opinion. However, the Court said that expert evidence of human conduct in the psychological and physical factors which may lead to certain behaviour relevant to credibility is admissible, provided the testimony goes beyond the ordinary experience of the trier of fact. *Marquard* was charged with the aggravated assault of her three and a half year old grand-daughter. It was alleged that she had put the child's face against a hot stove door in order to discipline her. The child's unsworn testimony was that her "nana" had put her in (or on) the stove. Both the accused and her husband had testified that they discovered the child early in the morning, screaming, after she had burned herself trying to light a cigarette with a butane lighter. Among the expert testimony called by both the Crown and the defence was a witness who commented on the child's credibility.

The Court said that the testimony of an expert as to why children may lie to hospital staff about the cause of their injuries was clearly admissible because the witness was an expert in child behaviour. A lay jury needed expert evidence to understand the full implication of the witness's change in story. The court said, however, that when the expert testified that she personally did not believe the first story of the child, preferring the second version which the child told at trial, she crossed the line between expert testimony and human behaviour and assessment of credibility of the witness herself.

---

[23] (1994), 25 C.R. (4th) 1, 85 C.C.C. (3d) 193 (S.C.C).

Again in *Burns*,[24] the Supreme Court reaffirmed that the use of experts to explain human behaviour is now clearly admissible to furnish the court with scientific information which is likely to be outside the experience and knowledge of the judge and jury. The Court said that the behaviour of a person who has been systematically abused is an example of a matter on which experts may assist. Moreover, the fact that such evidence is inadmissible for one purpose (i.e. to show the truthfulness of a witness) does not automatically prevent it being received for another legitimate purpose (i.e. to show whether the complainant was sexually abused).

Burns was charged with indecently assaulting the complainant when she was nine and sexually assaulting her when she was 16. The charges came to light when the complainant was, herself, convicted of sexually abusing young boys that she was baby-sitting and ordered to take counselling. At that time she revealed that she had been sexually abused. At the accused's trial, she said that she did not reveal the assaults when they occurred because the accused was a good friend of her father and she feared that she would be disbelieved and lose her father. Her psychiatrist testified as to her condition as a consequence of what she had undergone, giving a picture of why she reacted as she did.

On appeal, the accused's counsel argued that the psychiatrist's evidence went to the very root of the issue before the judge—that she had been sexually abused by the accused—which the court had to decide and usurped the function of the trial judge. The Supreme Court disagreed. It said that the fact that such testimony was admissible to explain human behaviour did not render it inadmissible just because it also violated the rule against oath helping and the very issue which the jury was required to decide, that is, whether the complainant was sexually abused.

4. OPINION AS TO THE CREDIBILITY OF THE ACCUSED

The general rule is that the Crown is not entitled to call either experts or lay persons to give opinion evidence that the accused is not a credible witness unless the accused puts his character in issue in which case only character evidence may be called in reply. Nor

---

[24] (1994), 29 C.R. (4th) 113, 89 C.C.C. (3d) 193 (S.C.C.).

is the Crown allowed to lead in chief expert opinion about the accused's disposition to commit a crime unless it is relevant to an issue and is not being used merely as evidence of disposition.[25] The same rule applies to prevent an accused from calling experts and laymen to give their opinion that he is a credible witness. However, in the last twenty-five years, some authorities have allowed experts to testify as to the disposition or propensity of the accused to commit or not commit certain acts where they are relevant to a fact in issue. Unfortunately, these authorities have failed to clearly state the principles governing the admission of such evidence.

For example, in *Lupien*,[26] the Supreme Court of Canada said that an expert could testify that an accused lacked homosexual propensities to support the accused's evidence that he had did not know that his companion who was dressed as a women was, in fact, a man. Similarly, in *McMillan*,[27] an accused charged with the murder of his child was allowed to call an expert to testify that his wife had the disposition to commit the murder. A closer examination of both these cases reveals that the evidence was admitted more to demonstrate lack of propensity of the accused rather than to support his credibility.

However, in *Dietrich*,[28] the Ontario Court of Appeal, relying on the authority of *Lupien*, permitted an expert to testify that the accused had a psychopathic personality with a propensity for confessing to things that he did not do and should be believed when he testified that his confession was false. Although *Dietrich* says that an expert may give evidence bolstering the credibility of an accused, the expert testimony, in effect, also went to the issue of the propensity of the accused, this time to his propensity to confess to things that he did not do.

Recently, the Supreme Court of Canada stressed in *Mohan*[29] that evidence of an expert witness that the accused, by reason of his or her mental make-up or condition of the mind, would be incapable of committing, or disposed to commit, the crime is limited in scope. The Court noted that although the exception has been

---

[25] *Mohan, supra*, note 5.
[26] *Supra*, note 10.
[27] (1976), 23 C.C.C. (2d) 160 (Ont. C.A.).
[28] (1970), 11 C.R.N.S. 22, 1 C.C.C. (2d) 49 (Ont. C.A.).
[29] *Supra*, note 5.

applied to abnormal behaviour connoting sexual deviance, its under-lying rationale was based on distinctiveness.

In *Mohan*, Sopinka J., delivering the judgment of the Court, said that before an expert's opinion as to disposition may be admit-ted as evidence, the trial judge must be satisfied, as a matter of law, that either the perpetrator of the crime or the accused has distinc-tive behavioural characteristics such that a comparison of one with the other will be of material assistance in determining innocence or guilt. Although this decision is made on the basis of common sense and experience, it is must not be made in a vacuum. The trial judge must determine whether the expert is merely expressing a per-sonal opinion or whether the behavioural profile which the expert is putting forward is in common use as a reliable indicator of mem-bership in a distinctive group. A finding that the scientific commu-nity has developed a standard profile for the offender who commits this type of crime will satisfy the criteria of relevance and neces-sity. The evidence will qualify as an exception to the exclusionary rule relating to character evidence provided the trial judge is satis-fied that the proposed evidence is within the field of expertise of the expert witness.

In *Mohan*, the defence of the accused, a doctor charged with sexually assaulting four female patients aged 13 to 16, was that what the patients said was not true. The trial judge had refused to allow the defence to call a psychiatrist who would say that the offences had unusual features that would indicate that a physician who com-mitted them was a member of one or the other of an unusual and limited class and, that in his opinion, the accused was not a mem-ber of either class. It was held that the trial judge was correct in not allowing the admission of such evidence. There was no body of evidence that doctors who commit sexual assaults fall into a dis-tinctive class with identifiable characteristics.

7

Admissions and Confessions

1. THE RULE

A confession is defined as a statement either in writing or given orally by a person accused of a crime that shows or tends to show that he is guilty of the crime with which he is charged. An admission is said to be distinguishable from a confession because it is only an acknowledgment of a material fact that may form a link in the chain of proof against the accused. Unlike a confession, an admission need not necessarily be in writing or made orally; it can also include conduct that could reasonably be taken to be intended as an assertion.[1] The simplest example of an admission by conduct is when a police officer asks the accused if the murder weapon belongs to him and the accused nods his head affirmatively. No words have been spoken, but his conduct is sufficient to constitute an admission that the weapon belongs to him.

Some legal scholars regard admissions and confessions as exceptions to the hearsay rule; others say that they are not because they are not offered to prove a fact in issue, but only to impeach the credibility of the accused. The first view is probably correct. Admissions and confessions are exceptions to the hearsay rule because

---

[1] *St. Lawrence* (1949), 7 C.R. 464, 93 C.C.C. 376 (Ont. H.C.).

it is only logical to assume that what a person says against his own interest is probably true.

The distinction between a confession and an admission is not important when it comes to the rule relating to their admissibility. Both are governed by the same rule which was stated by Lord Sumner in *Ibrahim*[2] and judicially endorsed in Canada by the Supreme Court of Canada in *Boudreau*,[3]

> It has long been established as a positive rule of English criminal law, that no statement by an accused is admissible in evidence against him unless it is shown by the prosecution to have been a voluntary statement, in the sense that it has not been obtained from him either by fear of prejudice or hope of advantage exercised or held out by a person in authority. The principle is as old as Lord Hale.

There are three reasons for this rule. The first is the concern that a confession following an inducement may be false. The second reason is a more emotional one. Until the middle of the seventeenth century, it was a common practice for the Ecclesiastic Courts to compel anyone suspected of committing a crime against the security of the state to attend before a government official and to require him to take an oath, called the *ex officio* oath, to tell the truth to all questions that might be put to him. He was not told of the specific crime nor the names of the witnesses. If he told the truth, he might find himself charged with a crime that would put his life in peril. If he lied, he was charged with perjury and imprisoned. If he said nothing, he was arrested, tortured and incarcerated. It was not until the famous *Lilburne* case[4] in 1641 that the *ex officio* oath was abolished and it was recognized that no man should be required to incriminate himself — "nemo tenetur prodere se ipsum" or" nemo tenetur prodere accusare".

There is a third reason why the courts will reject a confession that has been obtained under circumstances which indicate that it is not voluntary. It is important that the public have confidence in the way that police carry out their duty to investigate crime. Unless the court is satisfied that the confession of an accused is free and voluntary, there is the concern that the public will believe that oppressive tactics are regularly used by the police. This will result

---

[2] (1914) A.C. 599.
[3] (1949), 7 C.R. 427, 94 C.C.C. 1 (S.C.C.).
[4] (1649), 4 St. Tr. 1270.

in a loss of support and respect by the community for the criminal justice system.

2. FORMAL ADMISSIONS

At common law, an accused was not permitted to make a formal admission where he was charged with a felony; nor is it certain that he could even do so where the charge was a misdemeanour. Section 655 of the *Criminal Code*[5] has altered that rule. It permits an accused charged with an indictable offence to "admit *any fact* alleged against him for the purpose of dispensing with proof thereof."

Does section 655 permit the defence to admit the voluntariness of a confession? The voluntariness of a confession is a question of law and is, strictly speaking, not something that can be admitted because section 655 only permits admissions of fact. However, trial judges have been able to get around this dilemma by having the accused admit that all of the facts leading up to the taking of the statement are consistent with it being voluntary.

Although the admission is characterized as a factual one, it does have legal consequences. However, in *Park*,[6] the Supreme Court of Canada went so far as to suggest that the defence has the right to waive the usual *voir dire* held to consider the voluntariness of the statement, and the trial judge has the wide discretion to accept that waiver if he is satisfied that the statement is voluntary.

3. ADMISSIONS BY CONDUCT

If we can assume that what a person says against his own interest is probably true and should be admitted against him, it follows that how he responds when an incriminating statement is made in his presence should be admissible against him if his actions or conduct are indicative of guilt.

Let us assume, for example, that Constable Jones, who is investigating a charge of assault, confronts the accused Brown and tells him that he has reasonable grounds to believe that he has just assaulted Smith. If Brown responds by punching the officer and

---

[5] R.S.C. 1985, c. C-46.
[6] (1981), 21 C.R. (3d) 182, 59 C.C.C. (2d) 385 (S.C.C.).

running away, it would be natural to assume that his conduct is indicative of guilt and should be admissible against him. However, if Brown responds by denying the charge, as one would expect an innocent person to do, then his denial is not admissible at the instance of the defence because it is self-serving. This contradiction is often difficult to accept.

Silence of the accused creates another problem. Although silence in the face of an accusation might cause one to ask why an innocent person has not denied his guilt, the law does not permit the Crown to lead evidence of the accused's silence in the face of an accusation. The reason is that an accused's right to silence is a constitutional guarantee. Thus, it would be a delusion and unfair for the police to caution an accused that he has the right to remain silent and then use that silence in the face of a question that suggested his guilt.[7]

The problem arises because in *Christie*,[8] it was held by the House of Lords that in some circumstances even a denial of an accusation might amount to an acknowledgement of its truth. One might question how a denial of an accusation could ever amount to an adoption of it unless the denial turns out to be an untrue statement. If this occurs, the prosecution might be able to use the denial to attack the accused's credibility to show that it is inconsistent with a prior or subsequent statement made by him.

The real difficulty arises where the accused's response is ambiguous and open to interpretation. Should the trial judge refuse to admit the response, or should he admit it and leave it to the jury to draw their own conclusions? Unfortunately, the courts have offered little guidance. For example, in *Fargnoli*,[9] the accused was arrested for indecently assaulting his daughter and, when asked whether he wished to say anything, replied, "You got it all there... there is nothing more for me to say about it." Two members of the Ontario Court of Appeal held that the response amounted to an acceptance of the facts while the third dissented, holding that the response was ambiguous and ought not to have been admitted.

---

[7] *Chambers* (1991), 80 C.R. (3d) 235, 59 C.C.C. (3d) 321 (S.C.C.).
[8] [1914] A.C. 545.
[9] (1957), 25 C.R. 310, 117 C.C.C. 359 (Ont. C.A.).

4. THE MEANING OF VOLUNTARY

If one applies the *Ibrahim* rule strictly, it means that no statement can be admitted if it was obtained as a result of a threat or a promise. The law does not require that the threat be openly made. Words or conduct which would lead an accused to believe that violence will be used on him if he does not confess will amount to threat. Even a veiled promise of punishment will amount to a threat. This is why it is important for the judge to look at all of the surrounding circumstances before he considers the effect of the words or conduct of the police officer.

Phrases such as "it would be better for you if you told us what happened", or "you will be arrested if you do not tell us where the stolen goods are", or "you had better tell us the truth", or "it is necessary to give an explanation" have been held to be a threat; whereas words such as "be sure to tell the truth" and "be a good girl and tell the truth" have been held not to constitute a threat. The reason is that the first group of words are an expression of compulsion or obligation to speak whereas the second are not. However, the dividing line is difficult to draw and this why it is important to look at the context in which the specific words are used.

The background of the accused, himself, is also a relevant factor. Someone who has never been involved with the police before may be so terrified by the predicament in which he finds himself that he may be more influenced by suggestions made by a police officer than an experienced criminal would be.

The promise or inducement is anything that gives the accused some hope or expectation with respect to the charge or contemplated charge, or some other matter. That "some other matter" could be another charge against the accused or a charge against someone whom the accused might wish to help such, as his wife or child, or a close friend. A promise or inducement could result, not only from the police officer's words, but also from a combination of his words and those of the accused. For example, if an accused asked a police officer whether he would be released "if I give a statement", the officer's affirmative reply could constitute an inducement. Any suggestion by a police officer that he will offer the accused assistance could constitute an inducement if it evokes a confession from the accused.

For forty years after *Ibrahim*, the courts applied the rule so strictly that exclusion occurred only where there was an actual threat or inducement. However, in 1956, the Supreme Court of Canada in *Fitton*[10] finally recognized the role which compulsion or oppression could play in causing someone to make a statement. Mr. Justice Rand expressed it this way,

> The rule on the admission of confession... at times presents difficulty of application because its terms tend to conceal underlying considerations material to a determination. The cases of torture, actual or threatened, or of unabashed promises are clear; perplexity arises when more subtle elements must be evaluated. The strength of mind and will of the accused, the influence of custody or its surroundings, the effect of questions or of conversation, all call for delicacy in appreciation of the part they have played behind the admission, and to enable a court to decide whether what was said was freely and voluntarily said, that is, was free from the influence of hope or fear aroused by them.

This passage recognizes that oppressive conditions may cause a person to feel compelled to make a confession. Oppressive conditions have a tendency to sap a person's free will, which is a necessary element of a voluntary confession. Since each individual has a unique psychological make-up, the court must examine all of the conditions surrounding the taking of the statement, such as the length of the period of questioning, the length of time intervening between periods of questioning, whether the accused was given proper refreshment, and the individual characteristics of the accused. As has been noted,

> What may be oppressive as regards a child, an invalid or an old man or somebody inexperienced in the ways of this world may turn out not to be oppressive when one finds that the accused person is a tough character and an experienced man of the world.[11]

It is important to stop at this stage and to observe that the focus of the traditional *Ibrahim Rule* was not upon any conscious choice of an accused whether to speak or not to speak to the police; his or her rights could be viewed only negatively in the sense that there was a right not to be tortured or coerced into making a statement by threats or promises held out by a person who was and whom the accused believed was a person in authority. In 1979, however,

---

[10] (1956), 24 C.R. 371, 116 C.C.C. 1 (S.C.C.).
[11] Note to *Martin Priestley* (1967), 51 Cr. App. R. 1.

the Supreme Court of Canada recognized for the first time that the
focus should also be on the accused's state of mind. In *Ward*,[12]
Mr. Justice Spence wrote,

> In my view, there is a further investigation of whether the statements were
> freely and voluntarily made even if no hope of advantage or fear of preju-
> dice could be found in consideration of the mental condition of the accused
> at the time he made the statements to determine whether or not the state-
> ments represented the operating mind of the accused.

Ward, who had been involved in a single car collision, was
found lying unconscious outside his vehicle. His lady friend was
found dead beside him. After being revived by mouth to mouth
resuscitation at the scene of the accident, Ward was questioned by
police officers but denied driving the vehicle. Thirty minutes later
and again some five or six hours later at the hospital, he was questioned and this time admitted driving the vehicle. He was charged
with criminal negligence.

On the *voir dire*, Ward said that he could not remember anything from the time that he was in a hotel some hours before the
accident until the afternoon or evening following the accident. His
doctor testified that he could answer simple questions but was unable
to tell them what happened. The Court held that the trial judge was
correct in excluding Ward's answers to the police officers because
they did not represent his "operating mind".

A similar result was reached in *Horvath*.[13] Horvath, a youth
of 17, was charged with the murder of his mother. On the evening
of his arrest, he was interrogated and cross-examined by two police
officers for two and one-half hours, but the statement he gave contained nothing inculpatory. The next day, he was interviewed by
another officer, a skilled interrogator, for four hours except for
three brief intervals. Horvath, who was left alone during those three
intervals, was observed by the officer reflecting aloud in what were
called "monologues" or "soliloquies". During the second monologue, he admitted killing his mother and repeated the confession
to the officer. In the third monologue, he asked his mother's forgive-
ness for having disclosed the incident. He then signed a confession.

The trial judge, however, rejected the confession after accepting

---

[12] (1979), 7 C.R. (3d) 153, 44 C.C.C. (2d) 498 (S.C.C.).
[13] (1979), 7 C.R. (3d) 97, 44 C.C.C. (2d) 385 (S.C.C.).

the opinion of a psychiatrist that Horvath had been in a hypnotic state for a large part of the interview before he signed the confession. In a split decision of the Supreme Court of Canada, it was held that the confession, which had followed directly from the earlier statement, and which was made while under hypnosis, was not voluntary because it had been induced by conditions created earlier.

In 1986, the importance of the accused's subjective state of mind was expanded into a further consideration: whether the accused was aware of what was at stake in making any statement. In *Clarkson*[14] the accused, while intoxicated, had confessed to the police to murdering her husband. The trial judge excluded the statement because he was not satisfied that the accused was "aware of the consequences" of making the statement. His decision was upheld by the Supreme Court of Canada, but only two of the seven judges agreed with the trial judge's reasons. Although the remaining judges held that the accused had been deprived of her right to counsel, they did not reject the "awareness of the consequences" test. It was held that it was up to the trial judge, in his or her unique position of hearing all of the witnesses, to decide that issue by balancing the probative value of the evidence in the light of the possible prejudice to the accused.

The "awareness of the consequences" test means essentially that a statement made by an accused is not admissible if the accused is not aware that he or she is making a statement that may be used against him or her. *Clarkson* was a straightforward case involving an intoxicated accused. Is there any reason why the rule should be limited to persons in a similar situation?

Two subsequent decisions of the Supreme Court of Canada suggest that it should be. The first, *Hebert*[15] involved an accused who had refused to give a statement to the police after he had consulted counsel but who later unknowingly confessed to an undercover police officer who had been placed in his cell. Madame Justice McLachlin, who delivered the majority judgment of the Court, held that the confession to the undercover officer should be excluded because the accused's right to counsel had been infringed. In other words, by placing an undercover officer in his cell, the accused's right to remain silent, which is protected as a fundamental principle

---

[14] (1986), 50 C.R. (3d) 289, 25 C.C.C. (3d) 207 (S.C.C.).
[15] (1990), 77 C.R. (3d) 145, 57 C.C.C. (3d) 1 (S.C.C.).

of justice under section 7 of the *Canadian Charter of Rights and Freedoms*,[16] had been breached. This was because "The guarantee of the right to counsel confirms that the essence of the right is the accused's freedom to choose whether to make a statement or not."

Madame Justice McLachlin, however, went on to stress that,

> I should not be taken as suggesting that the right to make an informed choice whether to speak to the authorities or to remain silent necessitates *a particular state of knowledge on the suspect's part over and above the basic requirement that he possess an operating mind. The Charter does not place on the authorities and the courts the impossible task of subjectively gauging whether the suspect appreciates the situation and the alternatives.* Rather, it seeks to ensure that the suspect is in a position to make an informed choice by giving him the right to counsel. The guarantee of the right to counsel in the Charter suggests that the suspect must have the right to choose whether to speak to the police or not, but it equally suggests that the test for whether that choice has been violated is essentially objective.[17]

In other words, what she was stressing was that the mental element required by an accused before a confession will be accepted is that of an operating mind, the *Horvath* and *Ward* test. The *Clarkson* case was only referred to in her judgment in the context of the waiver of the right to silence.

The second case, *Evans*[18] involved a youth of subnormal intelligence who was charged with the brutal murder of two women. The police had suspected that the accused's older brother was involved in the killings and had arrested the accused on a charge of trafficking in marijuana in the hope that he would be able to provide evidence against his brother. When advised of his right to counsel and asked if he understood his rights, the accused said "no". During the course of his interrogation by the police, the accused became the prime suspect in the murders, but was not told that he was being detained for murder nor advised again of his right to counsel. It was held that statements taken from the accused were improperly admitted by the trial judge because the accused's right to counsel had been infringed. Madame Justice McLachlin, who again delivered the majority view, this time held,

---

[16] *Canadian Charter of Rights and Freedoms*, Part 1 of the Constitution Act, 1982, being Schedule B to the Canada Act 1982 (U.K.), 1982, c. 11.

[17] *Supra*, note 15 at p. 183.

[18] (1991), 4 C.R. (4th) 144, 63 C.C.C. (3d) 289 (S.C.C.).

> In view of the appellant's subnormal mental capacity and the circumstances surrounding his arrest — the fact that no attempt was made to explain his rights to him after he indicated that he did not understand them, as well as the fact that he was subjected to a day of aggressive and at times deceptive interrogation which apparently left him feeling as if he had "no choice" but to confess — *I am not satisfied that he appreciated the consequences of making the written statement and thereby waiving his right to counsel* or, to put it another way, that he waived his right "with full knowledge of the rights the procedure was enacted to protect and of the effect the waiver will have on those rights in the process.[19]

In other words, because of his subnormal mental capacity, the test was "an appreciation of the consequences of making the statement". This time, the *Clarkson*[20] case was cited as authority.

It would appear from *Hebert* and *Evans*, that the Supreme Court has drawn a distinction between those whose mental faculties are normal and those who are mentally incapacitated because of an inherited condition or one induced by alcohol (and possibly drugs). In the former, the threshold test for voluntariness is an operating mind, that is one who understands what he or she is saying, whereas in the latter, the threshold test is higher and includes not only one who understands what he or she is saying but also appreciates that what he or she is saying may be used against them.

5. PERSONS IN AUTHORITY

It may be remembered that the Ibrahim rule said that a confession of an accused is not admissible unless it is voluntary in the sense that it was not obtained by a threat or promise held out by "a person in authority." If the person is not someone in authority, then the rule does not apply and the confession will be admissible.

There are few authorities which clearly define who is or who is not a "person in authority". A number of cases, however, have held that certain people such as police officers, gaolers or guards, magistrates or judges, prosecutors, informants or complainants, employers and building inspectors are persons in authority. It may be said as a general rule that a person in authority will include any-

---

[19] *Ibid.*, at p. 164 (C.R.).
[20] *Supra*, note 14.

one who has authority or control over the accused or over the proceedings or prosecution against him.[21]

In *A.B.*,[22] Mr. Justice Cory (then a member of the Ontario Court of Appeal) reviewed a number of authorities and concluded that,

1. as a general rule, a person in authority is someone engaged in the arrest, detention, examination or prosecution of the accused; the word "examination" refers to interrogation by police officers, detention or security guards and members of the Crown Attorney's office.
2. in some circumstances, the complainant in a criminal prosecution may be considered to be a person in authority.
3. the parent of an infant who is the injured party or a complainant in a criminal prosecution may be a person in authority, depending upon the factual background.
4. an inducement made by one who is not a person in authority, but made in the presence of persons in authority, may be deemed to have been made by a person in authority; in other words, a person not in authority is clothed with that authority by the presence of those in authority.

On the other hand, persons such as physicians, surgeons and psychiatrists, the father or wife of the accused, or a friend, have been held not to be persons in authority. However, in some instances someone such as a doctor or a psychiatrist who is called in by the Crown to examine the accused may be considered a person in authority if he pursues an active role in questioning the accused for the purpose of obtaining an admission or confession.

For a long time, a perplexing question was whether a subjective or an objective test should be used in determining if the person was someone "in authority". In other words, was it enough that the person was someone in authority or was it necessary for the accused to believe as well that he was a person in authority? One would have thought that the answer was self-evident, at least in the case of an inducement. How can a person be affected by an inducement unless he believes that the person has the ability to make good his promise? However, the case of a threat or a beating would be

---

[21] *Todd* (1901), 4 C.C.C. 514 (C.A.).
[22] (1986), 26 C.C.C. (3d) 17 (Ont. C.A.).

another matter. Here a confession would be rejected by a trial judge in exercise of his discretionary power to prevent the administration of justice from being brought into disrepute rather than from the rules relating to persons in authority.

Nevertheless, that question was never settled until the decision of the Supreme Court of Canada in *Rothman*.[23] There the court held that the test was a subjective one. The real issue was whether the accused thought that the person to whom he confessed could either make good his promise or carry out his threats. Thus, if the accused confessed to someone such as an undercover officer, then that officer was not a person in authority even though he might be, from a purely objective point of view, considered to be in a position of undoubted authority.

6. ONUS OF PROOF

Where the prosecution seeks to introduce a confession or admission, the trial judge will generally conduct a voir dire, that is a trial within a trial, and exclude the jury while he considers the voluntariness of the statement. On the *voir dire*, the prosecution is entitled to call evidence to establish the voluntariness of the statement. The defence is entitled to cross-examine the prosecution witnesses and to call witnesses on behalf of the defence including the accused who may, in turn, be cross-examined by the prosecution. After hearing argument from both sides, the judge will decide whether the statement should be admitted.

If the accused elects to testify on the *voir dire*, he may be cross-examined on the particular issue in dispute, that is, whether the statement is voluntary. This has been held to include the right to ask him whether the confession is true because it goes to the issue of his credibility.[24] This decision of the Supreme Court of Canada has been strongly criticized because it does "under the guise of 'credibility'... transmute what is initially an inquiry as to 'admissibility' of the confession into an inquisition of an accused."[25]

Moreover, the argument that the prosecution should be allowed to test an accused's credibility, by asking him on a *voir dire* whether

---

[23] (1981), 20 C.R. (3d) 97, 59 C.C.C. (2d) 30 (S.C.C.).
[24] *DeClercq* (1969), 4 C.R.N.S. 205, [1969] 1 C.C.C. 197 (S.C.C.).
[25] *Hnedish* (1958), 39 C.R. 347 (Sask. Q.B.), at pp. 349-50.

the confession is true, is a double edged sword. If he denies the truth of the statement, is he to be disbelieved simply because he contradicts the testimony of the police? On the other hand, if he admits that the confession is true, is he to be disbelieved when he says that it was obtained by threats or inducement? One could argue more persuasively that if he admits that the confession is true, this tends to show that he is telling the truth and should be believed when he says that the police used violence or inducements to obtain it from him. Moreover, if he does admit that the confession was true, this places the trial judge in the difficult position of having to exclude an important piece of evidence obtained under circumstances which the administration of justice does not condone, even though he knows that it is true.

The onus of proof lies upon the Crown to satisfy the court beyond a reasonable doubt that the statement is voluntary in the sense described earlier. It is not enough for the prosecution to simply call the interrogating officers, establish that the confession was preceded by the usual caution or warning, and then have the officers who took the statement say that it was made freely and voluntary.[26] The general rule is that the prosecution must call all persons who had anything to do with the accused during the period before the statement was made and during his interrogation, or at least make them available for cross-examination.[27]

There is no requirement that a confession be admitted only after a *voir dire* where the Crown has established the voluntariness of the statement beyond a reasonable doubt. In *Park*,[28] the Supreme Court of Canada recognized that an accused or his counsel could waive or dispense with the holding of a *voir dire* where the voluntariness of a confession was not in dispute. The decision whether or not to hold a voir dire lies with the trial judge. He may, if he is satisfied that no objection is taken to the admission of the statement without a *voir dire* and that voluntariness is not in issue, admit the statement without a voir dire.

---

[26] *Sankey* (1927), 48 C.C.C. 97 (S.C.C.).
[27] *Thiffault* (1933), 60 C.C.C. 97 (S.C.C.).
[28] (1981), 21 C.R. (3d) 182, 59 C.C.C. (2d) 385 (S.C.C.).

7. THE RIGHT TO COUNSEL

Section 10 of the *Charter* guarantees everyone the right… on arrest or detention,

(a) to be informed promptly of the reasons therefore;
(b) to retain and instruct counsel without delay and be informed of that right…

Whenever an accused is detained or arrested, he must be informed of his right to retain and instruct counsel. Except in the case of a youthful offender, the mentally or physically infirm, and possibly someone who has had no experience with the police, that duty is simply to advise the accused of his right to counsel and to provide him with the opportunity to contact his lawyer if he requests. He is not required to satisfy the court that the detained or arrested person understood his rights unless there are circumstances that would lead him to believe otherwise. It is generally presumed that a person understands the meaning of the right to counsel unless that person can establish otherwise.[29]

Once a person, who has been advised of his right counsel, indicates that he wishes to exercise that right, the police officer questioning him must stop until that request is fulfilled.[30] If he ignores that request, any statement obtained will be excluded at trial under section 24(2) of the *Charter*.

However, an accused who requests the right to counsel cannot delay indefinitely consulting with him. He must take reasonable steps to try to contact his lawyer to obtain advice. If he fails to do so, then the police may proceed to question him.[31]

A person may waive his right to counsel and that waiver need not be in writing. However, the onus of establishing that the accused waived his right to counsel with full knowledge of the consequences of doing so lies upon the prosecution. That may be particularly onerous if it appears that the accused does not have his full faculties such as an accused who may be mentally ill, or was under the influence of drugs or alcohol.[32] In *Clarkson*, the Supreme Court of Canada held,

---

[29] *Anderson* (1984), 39 C.R. (3d) 193, 10 C.C.C. (3d) 417 (Ont. C.A.).
[30] *Manninen* (1987), 58 C.R. (3d) 97, 34 C.C.C. (3d) 385 (S.C.C.).
[31] *Tremblay* (1987), 60 C.R. (3d) 59, 37 C.C.C. (3d) 565 (S.C.C.).
[32] *Clarkson, supra,* note 14.

> While this constitutional guarantee cannot be forced upon an unwilling accused, any voluntary waiver in order to be valid and effective must be premised on a true appreciation of the consequences of giving up the right.

The police are not required to stop all questioning after an accused has consulted with his lawyer. They may question him provided that he is willing to be questioned. They are not required to advise his lawyer that they are about to question him because, presumably, the lawyer has advised his client of this right. The issue is really one of waiver. If an accused consents to be questioned after consulting a lawyer, then there is nothing objectionable in doing so. However, the prosecution must establish, as in any case where the right to counsel has been waived, that the accused agreed to the interrogation without the presence of his lawyer.

8. THE USE OF TRICKS

Should the courts condone the use of tricks by the police to obtain a confession? For example, is there anything wrong in placing a police officer, disguised in plain clothes and pretending to be a suspect under arrest, in a cell with an accused for the purpose of actively eliciting incriminating information, or even passively listening to what an accused may say? On the eve of the *Charter*, such conduct was not only accepted but was regarded as reasonably necessary for the pursuit of shrewd and sophisticated criminals.[33]

Almost a decade of the *Charter* has witnessed a reversal of that view. In *Hebert*[34] it was held that the right to silence had to be defined broadly enough to preserve for a detained person the right to choose whether to speak to the authorities or to remain silent. To permit the authorities to trick a suspect into making a confession to them after he or she has exercised the right of conferring with counsel and has declined to make a statement would permit the authorities to do indirectly what the *Charter* forbids them from doing directly. To do so would effectively deprive a suspect of that choice.

In *Hebert*,[35] statements made by the accused to a plainclothes officer posing as a suspect under arrest were excluded because

---

[33] *Rothman, supra*, note 23.
[34] *Supra*, note 15.
[35] *Ibid.*

the accused had said, after he had consulted counsel, that he did not wish to make a statement. The Court said that the police violated his right to remain silent by using a trick to negate his decision. However, the Court also stressed that the scope of the right to silence does not go so far as to prohibit the police from obtaining confessions in all cases. The right to silence was subject to the following limits:

1. There is nothing that prohibits the police from questioning an accused or a suspect in the absence of counsel after he has retained counsel. Police persuasion, short of denying the suspect the right to choose or of depriving him of an operating mind, does not breach the right to silence.
2. The right applies only after detention.
3. The right does not affect voluntary statements made to cellmates. The violation of the suspect's rights occurs only when the Crown acts to subvert the suspect's constitutional right to choose not to make a statement to the authorities.
4. A distinction must be made between the use of undercover agents to observe the suspect, and the use of undercover agents to actively elicit information in violation of the suspect's choice to remain silent.
5. Even where a violation of the suspect's right is established, the evidence may, where appropriate, be admitted. Only if the court is satisfied that its reception would bring the administration of justice into disrepute can the evidence be rejected under section 24(2) of the *Charter*. Where the police have acted with due care for the suspects rights, it is unlikely that the statements they obtain will be held inadmissible.

Cases that have followed *Hebert* have made it clear that not every admission made by an accused to a cellmate will be excluded as violating his right to counsel. The right to silence prohibits the police from actively eliciting statements from a detainee so as to infringe his right to silence. It does not apply where a police informer has been placed in the accused's cell to obtain incriminating statements from the accused so long as he acts independently of the police.[36] Nor will it apply where the admission is made to an under-

---

[36] *Johnston* (1991), 5 C.R. (4th) 185, 64 C.C.C. (3d) 233 (Ont. C.A.); *Gray* (1991), 66 C.C.C. (3d) 6 (Ont. C.A.).

cover officer who is placed in the accused's cell so long as the undercover officer does not actively elicit information from the accused.[37]

---

[37] *Graham* (1991), 3 C.R. (4th) 44, 62 C.C.C. (3d) 128 (Ont. C.A.).

PART C

Proof at Trial

8

Proof

1. GENERALLY

The common law system is known as the adversary or accusatorial system as opposed to the continental system which is described as the inquisitorial system. Although both systems have many characteristics in common, such as an oral hearing with both the prosecution and the accused separately represented by counsel and with no compulsion upon the accused to answer questions, there are distinct differences. Under the inquisitorial system, the judge takes an active role in questioning witnesses for the prosecution and in examining the accused and witnesses for the defence. Moreover, prior to trial, a brief or dossier compiled by a juge d'instruction or examining magistrate containing the examination of various witnesses is provided to the judge and jury.

The common law system may be more described as a duel between the Crown prosecutor and the defence counsel with the judge sitting in the middle as an impartial arbiter. There are, however, some limitations on the contestants. It is the duty of counsel for the Crown to bring out all of the facts both for and against the accused. Moreover, it has been said that,

> ... the business of counsel for the Crown is fairly and impartially to exhibit all the facts to the jury. The Crown has no interest in procuring a conviction. Its only interest is that the right person should be convicted, that the truth should be known, and that justice be done.[1]

On the other hand, it is the duty of counsel for the defence to use all of the legitimate means at hand to obtain an acquittal for his client.

The usual steps in the process are these: opening statement by the prosecution; presentation of the prosecution's case; opening statement by the defence; presentation of the evidence for the defence; rebuttal evidence by the prosecution; summation of counsel for the prosecution and for the defence; charge to the jury by the trial judge; verdict.

2. THE CASE FOR THE CROWN

(a) The Opening and the Evidence

In a jury trial, but not necessarily in a trial by judge alone, the prosecution will begin with an opening speech to the jury. The purpose of the speech is to lay before the jury a brief summary of the facts upon which the prosecution relies to establish its case and of the evidence that it expects each prosecution witness will give. The Crown must always be fair in the opening address as well as

---

[1] *Sugarman* (1935), 25 Cr. App. R. 109 (C.C.A.), at pp. 114-15.

in the prosecution in general. There is a duty to be impartial and to guard against injecting comments likely to excite or inflame the jury against the accused.

When the address of the prosecutor is completed, the trial judge will call upon the prosecution to present its case. Witnesses will then be called by the prosecutor to be examined in chief. In an examination-in-chief, the prosecution must be careful not to lead the witness on matters crucial to its case. A leading question is one which suggests the answer to the witness. For example, it is not permissible to ask the witness "Did you see the accused shoot the victim"? A leading question may also be one which takes for granted evidence that a witness has not yet given. The question "When did you stop beating your wife?" is leading because it assumes that the witness has already said that he beat his wife in the past and has stopped doing so.

(b) Confessions by the Accused

If the Crown intends to introduce a statement or admission made by the accused, it will indicate to the judge that a *voir dire* is required to determine the voluntariness of the statement or admission.[2] The defence may, however, be prepared to admit that the statement is voluntary in which case a *voir dire* is not necessary.[3] If the statement is ruled to be voluntary or admitted to be voluntary, then it will be introduced through the officer or person who took the statement and made an exhibit if it is in writing.

The Crown may not wish to introduce the statement because it is exculpatory, but use it to cross-examine the accused if he or she gives evidence contrary to the contents of the statement, or introduce it in reply. The courts, however, do not allow the Crown to lie in wait and permit the accused to trap himself.[4] Some courts have suggested that if the statement is relevant to a fact in issue, even if it does not directly incriminate the accused, the statement should be advanced as part of its case in chief. The only exception is where it is marginally, minimally or doubtfully relevant.[5] The

---

[2] *Piche* (1970), 12 C.R.N.S. 222, [1970] 4 C.C.C. 27 (S.C.C.).
[3] *Park* (1981), 21 C.R. (3d) 182, 59 C.C.C. (2d) 385 (S.C.C.).
[4] *Drake* (1970), 12 C.R.N.S. 220, 1 C.C.C. (2d) 396 (Sask. Q.B.).
[5] *Bruno* (1975), 27 C.C.C. (2d) 318 (Ont. C.A.).

more prevalent view is that although the Crown need not introduce the statement in chief, it must at least attempt to prove its voluntariness during the presentation of the prosecution case in chief.[6] If the statement is proved to be voluntary, this will at least alert the accused to the fact that it may be used by the Crown to cross-examine him if he gives testimony and his testimony conflicts with the contents of the statement.

(c) Introduction of Prior Testimony

If a witness gave evidence at the accused's preliminary hearing or at a previous trial of the accused on the same charge but now refuses to give evidence, or to be sworn, or is dead, insane, too ill to travel or testify, or is absent from Canada, section 715 of the *Criminal Code*[7] permits the witness' evidence to be read as evidence in the trial. However, section 715 also provides that the trial judge may refuse to permit the evidence to be read if the accused satisfies him that he did not have full opportunity to cross-examine the witness.

For some time, the courts felt that once the Crown complied with section 715, the judge was required to admit the transcript of the previous testimony. However, in *Potvin*,[8] the Supreme Court of Canada decided that a trial judge had the discretion to refuse to admit such evidence where it was obtained in a manner that was unfair to the accused. For example, the fact that a witness is absent from Canada will not necessarily result in the admission of the witness's testimony if the Crown could obtain his attendance by some minimal degree of effort. A judge might also refuse to permit the Crown to introduce transcript evidence if the Crown was aware at the time that the witness previously testified that he would not be available to testify at trial and failed to tell the defence so that they could use their best efforts to cross-examine him.[9]

---

[6] *Lizotte* (1980), 18 C.R. (3d) 364, 61 C.C.C. (2d) 423 (C.A. Qué.).

[7] R.S.C. 1985, c. C-46.

[8] (1989), 68 C.R. (3d) 193 (S.C.C.).

[9] *Kaddoura* (1987), 60 C.R. (2d) 393, 41 C.C.C. (3d) 371 (Alta. C.A.), leave to appeal to S.C.C. refused (1988), 64 C.R. (2d) xxx, 42 C.C.C. (3d) vi (note) (S.C.C.).

(d) No Case-Splitting by the Crown

The Crown is required to call all of its evidence to prove its case before the defence is called upon. This is known as the rule against case-splitting. It is based upon the principle that an accused should not be taken by surprise and need not incriminate himself until he has heard and thoroughly explored the entire case which the Crown intends to present against him. It has been said to provide " a safeguard against the importance of a piece of evidence, by reason of its late introduction, being unduly emphasized or magnified in relation to the other evidence".[10]

Although the rule requires the Crown to prove each and every element of the charge, it does not require the Crown to anticipate every defence which may be raised. For example, the Crown is not required to lead evidence in chief that could rebut an alibi of the accused, even if it has received notice from the defence prior to trial that the defence intends to introduce alibi evidence and has given particulars of that alibi.[11] Nor is the Crown required to lead evidence that an accused is not suffering from a mental disorder that would exempt him from criminal responsibility since section 16(2) of the *Code* provides that a person is presumed not to suffer from a mental disorder so as to be exempt from criminal responsibility "until the contrary is proved on the balance of probabilities".[12]

(e) Admissions by the Defence

The defence is entitled to admit a fact in issue thereby avoiding the necessity of the Crown proving the fact. Section 655 of the *Code* provides that where,

> an accused is on trial for an indictable offence, he or his counsel may admit any fact alleged against him for the purpose of dispensing with proof thereof.

---

[10] *Campbell* (1977), 1 C.R. (3d) 309, 38 C.C.C. (2d) 6 (Ont. C.A.), at p. 334, per Martin J.A. in Campbell.
[11] *Rafferty* (1983), 6 C.C.C. (3d) 72 (Alta. C.A.); *Andrews* (1979), 8 C.R. (3d) 22 (B.C. C.A.), leave to appeal to S.C.C. refused (1979), 28 N.R. 537n (S.C.C.).
[12] *Chaulk* (1991), 2 C.R. (4th) 1, 62 C.C.C. (3d) 193 (S.C.C.).

3. CROSS-EXAMINATION OF CROWN WITNESSES

(a) The Nature of the Cross-examination

When the prosecution has completed its examination-in-chief of a witness, the defence may cross-examine that witness. The purpose of cross-examination is to show that the witness is mistaken or lying, or it may be directed towards bringing out facts favourable to the defence which were not brought out in chief. Here, questions which suggest the answer are not only permitted, but will often be put to the witness by the cross-examiner.

The general rule is that questions on cross-examination must relate to a fact in issue or to the impeachment of the witness's credibility. This allows the cross-examiner to ask the witness questions not related to a fact in issue for the purpose of showing that the witness is a person of discreditable conduct on unrelated matters which have not or may not have resulted in a conviction. The purpose is to suggest that he should not be believed because of such bad character.[13] If the question is not relevant to a fact in issue or to the witness' credibility, the trial judge has the duty to disallow it even if the opposing counsel does not object.[14]

The trial judge also has the duty to prevent the cross-examiner from putting a question to the witness which is vexatious or has the effect of misleading or leaving a false impression with the court.[15] In *Rowbotham*,[16] Judge Borins described that duty this way,

> The trial judge may disallow any question put in cross-examination which may appear to him vexatious and not relevant to any matter proper to be inquired into, e.g., questions as to alleged improprieties of remote date or of such a nature as not seriously to affect present credibility. Thus, the trial judge may ask himself or herself in any particular situation whether the danger of unfair prejudice against the witness and the party calling him from character impeachment outweighs the probable value of the light shed on credibility. The court has a responsibility to ensure that witnesses are dealt with fairly and to prevent victimization. It is not the witness who is on trial. Counsel who proceeds on that premise frequently fails to assess the situation carefully.

---

[13] *Titus* (1983), 33 C.R. (3d) 17, 2 C.C.C. (3d) 321 (S.C.C.); *Gonzague* (1983), 34 C.R. (3d) 169, 4 C.C.C. (3d) 505 (Ont. C.A.).

[14] *Rowbotham* (1977), 2 C.R. (3d) 244, 33 C.C.C. (2d) 411 (Ont. G.S.P.); *Bourassa* (1991), 67 C.C.C. (3d) 143 (Que. C.A.).

[15] *Hehr* (1982), 24 Alta. L. R. (2d) 59 (Q.B.).

[16] *Supra*, note 14 at p. 299 (C.R.).

If the defence intends to introduce evidence contradicting the testimony of a witness on a fact in issue, it is generally recognized that counsel for the defence has an obligation during cross-examination to put the substance of that evidence to the witness so that the witness can have the opportunity of explaining the contradiction.[17] However, there is no hard and fast rule that it must always be done[18] and where it has failed to do so, the trial judge does not have the right to prevent the defence from leading that evidence in chief.[19] However, the failure to do so may adversely affect the defence when the jury retires to consider their verdict since they will generally be reminded by the trial judge that the witness was not given the opportunity of explaining the contradiction advanced by the accused or his witnesses. In other words, the failure to do so will generally go to the weight of the defence evidence on that issue, but not its admissibility.

(b) Questions as to Credibility — Rule Against Collateral Evidence

Questions in cross-examination which are directed only to the credibility of a witness and not a fact in issue are said to be collateral. The rule is that except for questions in cross-examination pertaining to the witness's previous criminal record, neither the defence nor the Crown are allowed to call evidence to refute the answer given by the witness. The reason why evidence to refute a witness on a collateral issue is not permitted, even though it may show that the witness is not a believable person, is because it is too remote and may distract the jury from the main issue in the case. Probably the main reason why such evidence is not permitted is because it would only encourage a series a mini-trials on the credibility of each witness and unduly prolong the length of the trial.

Occasionally a strict application of the rule will cause a miscarriage of justice and the courts will relax the strict enforcement of the rule. For example, in instances of alleged sexual abuse where there are no witnesses other than the victim and the accused, evidence that the victim has made other false allegation or has a history of telling habitual lies or of fantasizing is relevant to her general

---

[17] *Browne v. Dunn* (1893), 6 R. 67 (H.L.).
[18] *Mackinnon* (1992), 72 C.C.C. (3d) 113 (B.C. C.A.).
[19] *Palmer*, [1980] 1 S.C.R. 759.

credibility. Such evidence of refutation is often given by experts, such as psychiatrists, as opinion evidence rather than as an exception to the no collateral evidence rule.[20]

The practice of putting questions which are directed only to credibility and are collateral to the issues in the case can often be abused. A good example was the former practice by the defence in rape trials before the enactment of section 276 of the *Code* of asking the complainant whether she ever had sexual intercourse with a person other than the accused. The fact that the complainant had sexual intercourse with another male person who was not her husband was not then, nor is it now, relevant to the issue of whether she consented to intercourse with the accused. Nevertheless, the courts permitted the question under the guise that it tested her credibility. If the complainant denied it, the defence was not allowed to call evidence to refute it. It was collateral to the issue whether she consented to sexual intercourse with the accused and the defence was bound by her answer. Often the complainant did not know this. If she answered truthfully and admitted that she had, there was the concern that she would be judged on her morality rather than her credibility. Section 276 of the *Code* has now put an end to such practice unless the defence can establish that the question is relevant to a fact in issue.

(c) Previous Criminal Record of the Witness

The one exception to the rule against collateral evidence is section 12 of the *Canada Evidence Act*.[21] That section allows the cross-examiner to ask the witness (even an accused) whether he has ever been convicted of "any offence". If the witness denies the fact or refuses to answer, the opposite party is allowed to prove the conviction even though such evidence is strictly collateral to the facts in issue. The rationale underlying this section is that the question goes to the credibility of the witness. In other words, the fact that a witness (or the accused) has a criminal record goes to the issue of whether he is a credible witness. Presumably, it proceeds on the assumption that a person who has a criminal record is less likely to tell the truth than a person who does not. The risk of such

---

[20] *Gonzagne, supra*, note 13; *T. (S.)* (1986), 55 C.R. (3d) 321, 31 C.C.C. (3d) 1 (Ont. C.A.).
[21] R.S.C. 1985, c. C-5.

question in the case of the accused is that the jury may conclude that because the accused has been convicted of an offence on a previous occasion, he probably committed the offence before the court. The trial judge thus has the duty of instructing the jury that they must not draw this inference against the accused. The judge must also instruct the jury that they are only entitled to consider the record for the purpose of assessing the credibility of the witness (or the accused) with respect to the issue before the court.

The expression "conviction" used in section 12 has been interpreted to include the sentence imposed by the court so that the cross-examiner may question the witness about the penalty imposed.[22] The words "any offence" have been interpreted to mean any offence under a federal statute even though it does not truly relate to the criminal law power of the federal government.[23] The words also include convictions for offences committed outside of Canada so long as the process of adjudication of guilt is of a character that would constitute a conviction under Canadian law.[24]

4. THE REQUIREMENT FOR CORROBORATION

Although it is often said that the common law system is distinguishable from the civil law system because the court is entitled to reach a decision on the unsupported evidence of one witness, that is not the way it always was. In its infancy, the jury system required that a certain number of persons swear upon oath that an accused was guilty or not guilty, although it might be said that the witnesses were really giving evidence as to the accused's character rather than probative evidence on the question of his guilt or innocence. Later, as the jury system became more like what we know it to-day, certain rules developed. One was the requirement that no prosecution for treason could succeed upon the evidence of one witness; another was that a prosecution for perjury required clear corroborating testimony. A rule of practice also developed requiring the corroboration of the testimony of complainants in sexual cases, accomplices and children.

---

[22] *Boyce* (1975), 28 C.R.N.S. 336, 23 C.C.C. (2d) 16 (Ont. C.A.).

[23] *Watkins* (1992), 70 C.C.C. (3d) 341 (Ont. C.A.).

[24] *Stratton* (1978), 3 C.R. (3d) 289, 42 C.C.C. (2d) 449 (Ont. C.A.).

Support for the corroboration of women was based on the belief that,

>...these cases are particularly subject to the danger of deliberately false charges, resulting from sexual neurosis, fantasy, jealousy, spite or simply a girl's refusal to admit that she consented to an act of which she is now ashamed.[25]

For the corroboration of children, it was argued that,

>Children are suggestible and sometimes given to living in a world of make-believe. They are egocentric, and only slowly learn the duty of speaking the truth...a child's power of observation and memory tends to be even less reliable than that of an adult.[26]

In the last decade, the requirement for corroboration of the testimony of women, children and accomplices has been swept away either by legislation or case law.[27] In 1993, s. 659 of the *Criminal Code*[28] was amended to provide that,

>659. Any requirement whereby it is mandatory for a court to give the jury a warning about convicting an accused on the evidence of a child is abrogated.

The only surviving requirement for corroboration arises in prosecutions for treason (*Criminal Code* section 47(3)), perjury (*Criminal Code* section 133), forgery (*Criminal Code* section 367(2)), and procuring a feigned marriage (*Criminal Code* section 292(2)). This does not mean that apart from these offences, a judge is never required to warn the jury about evidence which may be suspect.

In *W.(R.)*,[29] Madame Justice McLachlin, in dealing with the evidence of children, noted

>The repeal of provisions creating a legal requirement that children's evidence be corroborated does not prevent the judge or jury from treating a child's evidence with caution where such caution is merited in the circumstances of the case. But it does revoke the assumption formerly applied to all children, often unjustly, that children's evidence is always less reliable than the

---

[25] Glanville Williams, *Proof of Guilt*, 3rd ed. (London: Stevens & Sons, 1963), at p. 159.
[26] *Ibid.*, at 178-179.
[27] *Vetrovec* (*sub. nom. R. v. Gaja*) (1982), 27 C.R. (3d) 304, 67 C.C.C. (2d) 1 (S.C.C.).
[28] S.C. 1993, c. 45, s. 9.
[29] (1992), 13 C.R (4th) 257, 74 C.C.C. (3d) 134 (S.C.C.).

evidence of adults. So if a court proceeds to discount a child's evidence automatically, without regard to the circumstances of the particular case, it will have fallen into an error.

Later she said,

> It is neither desirable nor possible to state hard and fast rules as to when a witness's evidence should be assessed by reference to "adult" or "child" standards — to do so would create anew stereotypes potentially as rigid and unjust as those which the recent developments in the law's approach to children's evidence have been designed to dispel. Every person giving testimony in court, of whatever age, is an individual, whose credibility and evidence must be assessed by reference to criteria appropriate to her mental development, understanding and ability to communicate. But I would add this. In general, where an adult is testifying as to events which occurred when she was a child, her credibility should be assessed according to criteria applicable to her as an adult witness. Yet with regard to her evidence pertaining to events which occurred in childhood, the presence of inconsistencies, particularly as to peripheral matters such as time and location, should be considered in the context of the age of the witness at the time of the events to which she is testifying.[30]

In *Vetrovec*,[31] Chief Justice Dickson suggested that what might be appropriate,

> ...in some circumstances, is a clear and sharp warning to attract the attention of the juror to the risks of adopting, without more, the evidence of the witness.

The need for some helpful direction, as he pointed out, was particularly important in lengthy trials where guilt or innocence would depend upon the acceptance or rejection of the evidence of one or more witnesses, or in cases involving accomplice evidence or disreputable witnesses.

As has been noted, there can be no conviction for treason, perjury, forgery or procuring a feigned marriage on the evidence of one witness unless that evidence is " corroborated in a material particular by evidence that implicates the accused." Corroborative evidence is thus independent confirmatory evidence of the witness which shows or tends to show not only that a crime was committed, but also that the accused committed it. The law is that the trial judge is required to specify for the jury what items of evidence are capa-

---

[30] *W. (R.), ibid.*, at pp. 267-268 (C.C.C.).
[31] *Supra*, note 27 at p. 17 (C.C.C.).

ble of being corroborative, leaving to them the ultimate question of deciding whether such items are, in fact, corroborative. If the items viewed cumulatively, (but not alone), are capable of constituting corroboration, the trial judge must specify those items which may be considered part of the cumulative package.[32]

5. RE-EXAMINATION OF A CROWN WITNESS

When the defence has completed the cross-examination of the witness, then Crown counsel will be permitted to re-examine the witness. The purpose of re-examination is to deal with new evidence or clarify matters raised by the defence during cross-examination. The Crown is not entitled to rehash or ask the witness to repeat evidence already given by him in chief.

6. REOPENING THE CROWN'S CASE

Occasionally, a prosecutor may discover that he has closed his case too soon and has omitted presenting evidence crucial to his case. He will then apply to the trial judge to be permitted to re-open his case. Whether or not he will be permitted to do so is a discretionary matter for the trial judge. Historically, three stages were recognized in the trial during which the discretion of the trial judge to allow the Crown to reopen its case could be exercised. The first stage was before the Crown closed its case. Here, the trial judge had a wide latitude in allowing the Crown to recall a witness to prove an omitted element of the case or correct earlier testimony. The second stage was after the Crown had closed its case. Here the trial judge had the discretion to allow the Crown to reopen its case to correct some oversight or prove a matter which it had failed to do so inadvertently, provided that there was no prejudice to the accused. However, once the defence had begun to present its case, the trial judge's discretion was narrowly restricted. The Crown was only allowed to reopen its case to prove a matter, *ex improviso*, which no human ingenuity could have foreseen.[33]

Allowing the prosecution to re-open its case after the defence was called upon to meet it was regarded as a indirect breach of the

---

[32] *McNamara (No.1)* (1981), 56 C.C.C. (2d) 193 (Ont. C.A.).
[33] *Cachia* (1974), 26 C.R.N.S. 302, 17 C.C.C. (2d) 173 (Ont. H.C.).

fundamental rule that an accused was not required to respond to the allegation until the Crown established that there was a "case to meet". Once there was a case to meet, then the accused could no longer remain passive and was required to answer the case against him or risk conviction.

However, in 1978, the Supreme Court of Canada seemed to sweep away these principles in *Robillard*[34] and indicate that there was absolutely no restriction on the trial judge's discretion. The Court said that the *ex improviso* rule did not apply to Canada and the trial judge had a wide discretion to allow the Crown to reopen its case even where the defence has been put to its election whether it intends to call evidence and has elected not to do so.

Very recently, the Supreme Court reconsidered its decision in *Robillard*. In *P.(M.B.)*,[35] the Court said that although Canadian jurisprudence has not applied the strict *ex improviso* rule as it has been applied at common law, the circumstances in which the Crown may be allowed to reopen its case, after the defence has begun its case, should be narrow and the *Robillard* case should be construed as applying only to situations where the Crown is seeking to reopen in order to correct a matter of form. The court gave three examples where a judge could exercise his discretion:

1. Where the conduct of the defence, either directly or indirectly, has contributed to the Crown's failure to adduce certain evidence before closing its case;[36]
2. Where the Crown's omission or mistake was over a non-controversial issue to do with purely formal procedural or technical matters, having nothing to do with the substance or merits of a case;[37]
3. Where the interests of the accused warrant reopening the Crown's case.[38]

---

[34] (1978), 41 C.C.C. (2d) 1 (S.C.C.).

[35] (1994), 29 C.R. (4th) 209, 89 C.C.C. (3d) 289 (S.C.C.).

[36] *Champagne*, [1970] 2 C.C.C. 273 (B.C. C.A.); *Crawford* (1984), 43 C.R. (3d) 80 (Ont. Co. Ct.).

[37] *Kissick* (1952), 14 C.R. 1, 102 C.C.C. 129 (S.C.C.); *Huluszkiw* (1962), 37 C.R. 386, 133 C.C.C. 244 (Ont. C.A.); *Assu* (1981), 64 C.C.C. (2d) 94 (B.C. C.A.).

[38] *Nelson*, [1993] O.J. No 1899 (Ont. Gen. Div.).

7. MOTION FOR DIRECTED VERDICT OR NO-CASE TO ANSWER

If the Crown has presented a *prima facie* case, then the trial judge will call upon the defence to present its case. However, the defence may ask the trial judge to direct the jury to return a verdict of acquittal on the basis that there is no case to answer. Where judge presides without a jury, the defence will ask the judge to enter a verdict of not guilty himself.

The test which the trial judge must apply in determining this issue is whether there is *any* evidence upon which a reasonable jury properly instructed could convict the accused. He must remember that at this stage of the proceedings, the question of proof beyond a reasonable doubt does not arise. Nor is he entitled to take the case away from the jury and direct them to render a verdict of acquittal because he concludes that the evidence is manifestly unreliable. In other words, he is not entitled to weigh the quality of the evidence even where he sits without a jury.

This does not mean that the judge never enters into a weighing process. His determination of whether there is any evidence to go to the jury requires him of necessity to weigh the evidence presented by the Crown to determine whether "a reasonable jury properly instructed could convict the accused." Since no reasonable jury could convict unless there was some evidence of substance, he must determine whether it is of sufficient quality to meet this threshold test. However, in assessing the quality of the evidence, what he must never do is to enter the province of the jury and decide whether the testimony of the witnesses is manifestly unreliable or, where the evidence is all circumstantial, whether that evidence is consistent with any conclusion other than the guilt of the accused. In a jury trial, the question of the weight of the evidence on the issue of proof beyond a reasonable doubt is for the jury not the judge, and he must be careful not to usurp their function. Although, one might wonder why the same rule applies in trials by judge alone where the judge is also the judge of the facts, the rule is still enforced strictly.

In *Monteleone*,[39] Mr. Justice McIntyre summed up the rule this way,

------

[39] (1986), 59 C.R. (3d) 97, 35 C.C.C. (3d) 193 (S.C.C.), at p. 103 (C.R.).

Where there is before the court any admissible evidence, whether direct or circumstantial, which, if believed by a properly-charged jury acting reasonably, would justify a conviction, the trial judge is not justified in directing a verdict of acquittal. It is not the function of the trial judge to weigh the evidence, to test its quality or reliability once a determination of its admissibility has been made. It is not for the trial judge to draw inferences of fact from the evidence before him. These functions are for the trier of fact, the jury.

Although some scholars have argued that a trial judge should go so far as to determine whether the evidence is sufficient to prove guilt beyond a reasonable doubt before it goes to the jury, that view fails to recognize and understand the different roles played by the judge and the jury in a criminal trial. They argue that such a threshold test ensures that section 7 of the *Charter of Rights and Freedoms*[40] which guarantees fundamental justice and section 11(d) which presumes everyone innocent until proven guilty, cannot be satisfied and given their full meaning.[41] It must be remembered, however, that the accused has chosen a jury, not a judge, to determine whether the Crown has established his guilt beyond a reasonable doubt and it must be assumed that the jury will obey the judge's instructions on this issue. To ask a judge to decide whether the Crown has established the guilt of the accused beyond a reasonable doubt before he allows the case to go to the jury carries the danger that if he allows the case to go to the jury, they might feel themselves compelled to agree with his decision on that issue and find the accused guilty even if they have a reasonable doubt. Moreover, even a finding of not guilty by a jury, in the face of a legal ruling by the judge that the evidence has established the accused's guilt beyond a reasonable doubt, might cause the public generally to feel that the administration of justice has been brought into disrepute.

If the judge agrees that there is no case to answer, he will direct the jury that, as a matter of law, they must acquit the accused. Even though his decision is a legal one, the rule until recently meant that once an accused had elected trial by jury and been placed in the jury's charge at the beginning of the trial, only the jury, not the judge, had jurisdiction to formally pronounce the verdict of not guilty and deliver him from that charge. This often placed the judge in an embarrassing position if the jury were reluctant to follow his

---

[40] *Canadian Charter of Rights and Freedoms*, Part 1 of the Constitution Act, 1982, being Schedule B to the Canada Act 1982 (U.K.), 1982, c. 11.
[41] See Annotation of David Tanovich, 27 C.R. (4th) 174.

instruction. In *Rowbotham*,[42] the Supreme Court of Canada decided to modify the rule and allow the judge to tell the jury that he was withdrawing the case from them and entering a verdict of acquittal. In trials by judge alone, the judge will simply render a verdict of not guilty and dismiss the charge.

8. THE CASE FOR THE DEFENCE

If there is some evidence upon which a jury properly instructed could convict the accused, the judge will call upon the defence to present its case. The defence may or may not call evidence. If the defence elects to call evidence, it is entitled to make an opening address to the jury. The purpose of the opening address is to outline to the jury essentially what the defence is all about and what the defence witnesses, including the accused if it is intended to call him, are expected to say.

If witnesses are called by the defence, the proceedings are reversed. The witnesses will be examined in chief by counsel for the defence, or the accused if he is unrepresented, cross-examined by counsel for the Crown and re-examined by counsel for the accused.

9. CROSS-EXAMINATION OF DEFENCE WITNESSES

(a) Generally

Although witnesses for the defence are open to the same kind of attack as witnesses for the prosecution, an accused who testifies occupies a special position when he is being cross-examined by Crown counsel. In *Davison*,[43] Mr Justice Martin succinctly summed up that position.

> An accused who gives evidence has a dual character. As an accused he is protected by an underlying policy rule against the introduction of evidence by the prosecution tending to show that he is a person of bad character, subject of course, to the recognized exceptions to that rule. As a witness, however, his credibility is subject to attack. If the position of an accused who gives evidence is assimilated in every respect to that of an ordinary wit-

---

[42] (1994), 30 C.R. (4th) 141, 90 C.C.C. (3d) 449 (S.C.C.).
[43] (1974), 20 C.C.C. (2d) 424 (Ont. C.A.), leave to appeal to S.C.C. denied, [1974] S.C.R. viii, at pp. 441-442.

ness he is not protected against cross-examination with respect to discreditable conduct and associations.

If the accused could in every case be cross-examined with a view to showing that he is a professional criminal under the guise of an attack upon his credibility as a witness, it would be virtually impossible for him to receive a fair trial on the specific charge upon which he is being tried. It is not realistic to assume that, ordinarily, the jury will be able to limit the effect of such a cross-examination to the issue of credibility in arriving at a verdict.

In my view the policy rule which protects an accused against attack upon his character lest it divert the jury from the issue which they are called upon to decide, namely, the guilt or innocence of the accused on the specific charge before the Court, is not wholly subordinated to the rule which permits an accused who elects to give evidence to be cross-examined on the issue of his credibility. In this area of the law, as in so many areas, a balance has been struck between competing interest, which endeavours so far as possible to recognize the purpose of both rules and does not give effect to one to the total exclusion of the other.

Consequently, limitations are imposed with respect to the cross-examination of an accused which do not apply in the case of an ordinary witness...

I conclude that, save for the cross-examination as to previous convictions permitted by section 12 of the *Canada Evidence Act*, an accused may not be cross-examined with respect to misconduct or discreditable associations unrelated to the charge on which he is being tried for the purpose of leading to the conclusion that by reason of his bad character he is a person whose evidence ought not be believed. Cross-examination, however, which is directly relevant to prove the falsity of the accused's evidence does not fall within the ban notwithstanding that it may incidently reflect upon the accused's character by disclosing discreditable conduct on his part.

On the other hand, where an accused gives evidence that is damning to the defence of a co-accused, the protection given by the *Davison* case does not apply if he is being cross-examined by a co-accused. In such instance, it is open for the co-accused to ask the accused questions about his character to show that he is a disreputable person not worthy of belief.[44] The policy of the law is that the right of an accused to full answer and defence does not allow him to hide under that umbrella of protection thereby impairing the right of his co-accused to full answer and defence by asking questions pertinent to his defence. If counsel for an accused who is being attacked by a co-accused perceives any prejudice as a result of the cross-examination of his client, he should apply to have his client's trial severed from his co-accused.

---

[44] *Jackson* (1992), 9 C.R. (4th) 57, 68 C.C.C. (3d) 385 (Ont. C.A.).

(b) Questions as to Credibility — Rule Against Collateral Evidence

As has already been pointed out, the general rule is that questions in cross-examination must relate to a fact in issue or to the impeachment of the witness's credibility. Except for questions pertaining to the witnesses's previous criminal record which may be proved pursuant to section 12 of the *Canada Evidence Act*, the only problem is that if a question is asked to test credibility but the question does not relate to a fact in issue, the Crown is not allowed to call evidence to refute the answer given by the witness. The prosecutor is bound by the answer.

One might question the wisdom of a rule that allows one side to ask a question to test credibility but does not allow evidence in reply to prove that the witness is being untruthful on that issue. The reason for the rule is to ensure that the trier concentrates on the issue in dispute and avoids a multiplicity of proceedings. If the cross-examiner were allowed to call impeachment evidence on every question that was put to a witness, it would mean that trials would be unduly prolonged while reply evidence was called to refute a witness's testimony.

(c) Criminal Record of the Accused

Section 12 of the *Act* provides that a witness (which includes the accused) "*may* be questioned as to whether he has been convicted of any offence" and, if he denies the fact or refuses to answer, the opposite party may prove the conviction. Here the word "conviction" has been strictly construed. Section 12 does not permit the Crown to go beyond prior convictions to cross-examine an accused as to discreditable conduct or association with disreputable individuals in order to attack his credibility.[45] Nor does it permit cross-examination where the accused was found guilty and granted a conditional discharge, the conditions being subsequently fulfilled.[46]

For some time, the law was uncertain as to whether the trial judge had any discretion to disallow the question where it was prejudicial to an accused, such as where the conviction was an old one, or where it bore no relationship to the issue of credibility (i.e.

---

[45] *Davison*, *supra*, note 44.
[46] *Danson* (1982), 66 C.C.C. (2d) 369 (Ont. C.A.).

convictions for dishonesty such as forgery, cheating and the like.).[47] It was argued that the word "may" in section 12 gave the judge the discretion to disallow the question in a proper case.[48] However, in *Stratton*,[49] the Ontario Court of Appeal concluded that there was no judicial discretion to exclude evidence rendered admissible by the section.

Eight years later, however, the Supreme Court of Canada in *Corbett*[50] in a split (4-2) judgment decided that a trial judge does have the discretion to exclude evidence of previous convictions of an accused in those cases where a mechanical application of section 12 of the *Act* would undermine the right of an accused to a fair trial as guaranteed by the *Charter*. The Court noted that a criminal record is a factor, to some extent, that bears on the credibility of a witness (or the accused). In other words, the fact that a witness has a criminal record does not mean that he should not be believed but is a factor that may be taken into account by the trier in assessing credibility. Since the prior record is only a factor to be considered in assessing credibility, section 12 did not, where the witness was the accused, infringe the presumption of innocence guaranteed by section 11(d) of the *Charter*.

Chief Justice Dickson, who delivered the main majority judgment, recognized that there was always a risk that a jury, if told that the accused had a criminal record, might make more of that fact than it should. On the other hand, he noted that there was also the risk that concealing the prior record of an accused who testified would deprive the jury of information relevant to credibility, and create a serious risk that they would be presented with a misleading picture. It was his view that the best way to balance and alleviate these risks was to give the jury all of the information, but at the same time require the trial judge to give them clear direction as to the limited use that they were to make of such information.

What factors should a trial judge consider in determining how the discretion should be exercised? Here Chief Justice Dickson indicated that he regarded those factors listed by Mr. Justice LaForest in his dissenting judgment as useful. Mr. Justice LaForest recog-

---

[47] *Morris* (1978), 43 C.C.C. (2d) 129 (S.C.C.), at p. 153.
[48] *Powell* (1977), 37 C.C.C. (2d) 117 (Ont. G.S.P.); *Skehan* (1978), 39 C.C.C. (2d) 196 (Ont. H.C.).
[49] *Supra*, note 25.
[50] (1988), 64 C.R. (3d) 1, 41 C.C.C. (3d) 385 (S.C.C.).

nized that it was impossible to provide an exhaustive catalogue of factors in assessing the probative value or potential prejudice of such evidence. He did, however, begin by indicating that he regarded the nature of the prior conviction as among the most important considerations. A conviction which involved acts of deceit, fraud, cheating or stealing was more probative of a person's honesty and integrity than an act of violence which had little or no direct bearing on a person's veracity. Another factor creating potential prejudice was the similarity of the prior conviction to the charge before the court.[51] As far as he was concerned, a trial judge should be wary of admitting such evidence unless it met the stringent test for admitting similar fact evidence. The remoteness or nearness of the previous conviction was also a factor to be considered. He was of the view that a conviction, even one involving an act of dishonesty, which occurred long before should be generally excluded on the grounds of remoteness.

One issue that gave Mr. Justice LaForest concern was the fairness to the Crown of prohibiting the cross-examination of the accused on prior convictions where the defence has made a deliberate attack upon the credibility of a Crown witness, particularly where the case boils down to a credibility contest between the accused and that witness. Although he was prepared to recognize that in such instance, the jury was entitled to have before it the record of the person attacking the character of the Crown witness in order to determine whether he was any more worthy of belief than the person attacked. He felt that this was not a factor that should override the concern for a fair trial.

10. REBUTTAL EVIDENCE FOR THE PROSECUTION

The general rule as to the order of proof is that the prosecution must introduce all evidence in its possession that it relies upon to establish its case before it closes its case. The rule is intended to prevent an accused from being taken by surprise, and to enable him to investigate by cross-examination the reliability of such evidence before he is called upon to introduce his defence. It is also intended to prevent the undue emphasis or magnification of

---

[51] *P. (G.F.)* (1994), 29 C.R. (4th) 315, 89 C.C.C. (3d) 176 (Ont. C.A.); *Trudel* (1994), 90 C.C.C. (3d) 318 (Que. C.A.).

evidence in relation to other evidence by reason of its late introduction.[52]

The Crown is not expected, however, to anticipate what the defence may be and to lead evidence to refute that defence in advance. For example, the Crown is not required to lead evidence in chief to rebut the defence of alibi, even where the defence has given notice that it intends to raise that issue when called upon. The Crown is entitled to wait until the defence has called its alibi evidence and lead its evidence by way of rebuttal.[53] Similarly, where the onus is upon the accused to raise the defence, such as in the case of mental disorder exempting from criminal responsibility, the Crown is not required to lead evidence of the mental disorder as part of its case in chief.[54]

Generally speaking, rebuttal evidence is restricted to evidence to meet new facts presented by the defence. But the accused's mere denial of the prosecution's case during the course of his testimony does not constitute new facts permitting the prosecution to repeat its case or to introduce additional evidence to support it. However, the trial judge does have the discretion to admit, in reply, evidence relevant to the Crown's case as a result of defence evidence which the prosecution could not reasonably be expected to anticipate.

An example where rebuttal evidence was introduced was *Sparrow* a murder case.[55] There the accused's car was found containing shell cartridges from the same type of gun used to kill the deceased. Blood stains from the same grouping as the deceased were also found on the car's trunk. During the course of his cross-examination, the accused "guessed" that the blood stains were as a result of a fist fight between the deceased and a friend several days before the killing. The Crown was allowed to call in reply a professor of "criminalistics" to testify as to the age of the blood stains because that issue was not a live one until the accused testified.

Atikian[56] is a good example of the Crown improperly splitting its case and calling, by way of rebuttal, evidence that should have been lead in chief. In that case, the parents of a 17 month old infant,

---

[52] *Campbell* (1978), 1 C.R. (3d) 309, 38 C.C.C. (2d) 6 (Ont. C.A.).
[53] *Andrews* (1979), 8 C.R. (3d) 22 (B.C. C.A.), leave to appeal to S.C.C. refused (1979), 28 N.R. 537n (S.C.C.); *Rafferty* (1983), 6 C.C.C. (3d) 72 (Alta. C.A.).
[54] *Chaulk* (1990), 2 C.R. (4th) 1, 62 C.C.C. (3d) 193 (S.C.C.).
[55] (1979), 12 C.R. (3d) 158, 51 C.C.C. (2d) 443 (Ont. C.A.).
[56] (1991), 3 C.R. (4th) 77, 62 C.C.C. (3d) 357 (Ont. C.A.).

who had died from malnutrition and bronchial pneumonia, were charged with failing, without lawful excuse, to provide the infant with the necessaries of life thereby causing her death. Their defence was that they were following the advice of a herbalist and honestly believed that this advice would restore their child to good health. After the defence completed its case, the Crown was allowed by the trial judge to call, by way of rebuttal, the accused's 16-year old daughter who had given to the police a prior statement in which she told them that her father did not believe in herbalists and that he was constantly urging her mother to take the baby to a doctor or to a hospital. It was held by the Ontario Court of Appeal that the trial judge erred in allowing the Crown to split its case this way. The reply evidence went to the very heart of the case. It was unfair to allow the Crown to lead that evidence in reply when neither parent had been confronted with their daughter's statement during cross-examination, nor given the opportunity to refute it.

As was pointed out in the previous section, rebuttal evidence is only allowed where the evidence relates to a fact in issue. The Crown is not allowed to call rebuttal evidence to contradict a collateral matter. Again, the purpose of the rule is to ensure that the trier of fact concentrates on the issue in dispute and is not sidetracked by a collateral matter. Thus, if an accused goes into the witness box and gives evidence about a matter that is not relevant to a fact in issue, he cannot be contradicted by evidence in reply. The Crown is bound by his answer.

Unfortunately, the rule allows an accused to go into the witness stand and make all kinds of unfounded allegations which cannot be refuted by evidence in reply. It does not mean that the trier has to accept the evidence given by the accused. It only means that the Crown cannot call evidence to directly contradict the accused on that issue.

An example of where this occurred is the *Krause* case.[57] In *Krause*, a murder case, it was alleged that the killing arose out of a drug deal between the accused and the deceased. At trial, the accused testified that it was a regular thing during the investigation for the police to take him down to the police station, that the police threatened to harass other drug dealers and say that they had been given the dealer's names by the accused, and that the police

---

[57] (1987), 54 C.R. (3d) 294, 29 C.C.C. (3d) 385 (S.C.C.).

showed him a gory photograph of the deceased on the first interview. The trial judge then permitted the Crown to call evidence by
way of rebuttal. On appeal to the Supreme Court of Canada, it
was held that evidence as to police integrity and their conduct in
relation to the accused during the investigation was collateral to
the main and only issue in the case, that is, whether the accused
killed the deceased and should not have been admitted by the trial
judge.

Recently, however, the Supreme Court has said that evidence
by way of reply need not be restricted solely to, and be determinative of, a fact in issue in the case, provided that it is related to an
essential issue.[58] Rebuttal evidence is admissible where it is related
to an essential issue which may be determinative of the case. If the
rebuttal evidence goes to an essential element of the case and the
Crown could not have foreseen that such evidence would be necessary, then it is generally admissible. In *Aalders*, the accused, who
was charged with first degree murder in the course of a break-in
at the victim's residence and theft of the victim's belongings, had
testified that the money found in his possession when he was arrested
came in part from his welfare allowance. By way of reply, the trial
judge had allowed the Crown to call two welfare workers to testify
that the accused had never received social assistance. It was held
that the trial judge had not erred in doing so, even though the
accused had admitted the robbery. Evidence as to the details of the
robbery formed an integral part of the Crown's case, and it was
important that any confusion with regard to the accused's statement and testimony on this essential issue be clarified. The Court
said that evidence from the welfare officials that the accused had
never received welfare payments was relevant and important because
it would establish that the robbery was, in all probability, the source
of all the money in his possession at the time of his arrest.

11. SURREBUTTAL BY THE DEFENCE

The general rule is that the Crown is allowed the last opportunity to call evidence and that is only in reply to new facts raised
by the defence which the Crown could not reasonably anticipate.
However, some recent cases have also extended this right of

---

[58] *Aalders* (1993), 21 C.R. (3d) 141, 82 C.C.C. (3d) 215 (S.C.C.).

rebuttal, or what might be more properly called surrebuttal, to the defence. But when we look closer at those authorities, we can see that they have not created new law. They have merely given the defence the right to rebut facts raised by the Crown for the first time in response to a defence which must be raised by an accused, such as a mental disorder which renders him incapable of appreciating the nature and quality of his act or omission or of knowing that it was wrong.

For example, in *Ewert*[59] the accused, who was charged with first degree murder, raised the defence of insanity and called a psychologist who testified that the accused was suffering from a particular disease of the mind. In reply, the Crown called three psychiatrists who said that the accused did not have that particular disease of the mind but had a psychopathic personality. Following that testimony, the accused sought to re-call its expert to reply to that evidence but was refused by the trial judge. It was held by the British Columbia Court of Appeal that since the Crown's evidence was not a denial of the thesis advanced by the defence but an alternative explanation of the accused's conduct, the rules regarding the permissible scope of surrebuttal must be applied liberally in order to allow the accused to make full answer and defence.

Similarly, in *Rhodes*,[60] the accused was charged with first degree murder based on an allegation of killing occurring during the commission of a rape. The defence called expert evidence to show that the accused did not suffer from a predisposition to engage in sexual assault. The Crown was allowed to call in rebuttal a witness who said that she had been raped by the accused two months before the killing occurred. It was held that since such reply evidence went to show the pre-disposition that the defence psychiatrist had rejected, the trial judge erred in refusing the accused the right to call witnesses in surrebuttal as to the rape allegations.

12. ADDRESSES OF COUNSEL AND THE JURY CHARGE

When all of the evidence is completed, counsel are entitled to address the jury or, in the case of trial by judge alone, the judge. The rule is that if the defence has called any evidence, including

---

[59] (1990), 52 C.C.C. (3d) 280 (B.C. C.A.).
[60] (1981), 21 C.R. (3d) 245, 59 C.C.C. (2d) 426 (B.C. C.A.).

the accused, the defence is required to address the jury or judge first. If the defence has called no evidence, then the usual practice is for the Crown, at the conclusion of its case, to address the jury or judge, and this will then be followed by counsel for the defence.

In his charge to the jury, the judge is required to review the evidence with them and instruct them on the law which they are to apply to that evidence. He will, of course, stress that while they are the sole judges of the facts and the weight to be given to the evidence presented, he is the final judge of the law and they must take their law from him. Upon the completion of his charge, the jury will then retire to consider their verdict.

In the case of a judge alone, the judge may deliver his verdict at the conclusion of argument by counsel or he may reserve and deliver his judgment at a future time.

9

Presumptions and Burdens of Proof

1. PRESUMPTIONS GENERALLY

Everyone involved in the field of criminal law knows that there is a presumption that a person accused of a crime is presumed innocent, and that there is a burden of proof upon the Crown to establish the guilt of an accused beyond a reasonable doubt. These well known examples of presumptions and burdens of proof, however, do not easily explain the distinction between the two.

An instructive definition was offered by Chief Justice Dickson of the Supreme Court of Canada in *Oakes*,[1]

> In determining the meaning of these words, it is helpful to consider in a general sense the nature of presumptions. Presumptions can be classified into two general categories: presumptions without basic facts and presumptions with basic facts. A presumption without a basic fact is simply a conclusion which is to be drawn until the contrary is proved. A presumption with a basic fact entails a conclusion to be drawn upon proof of the basic fact... Basic fact presumptions can be further categorized into permissive and mandatory presumptions. A permissive presumption leaves it optional as to whether the inference of the presumed fact is drawn following proof of the basic fact. A mandatory presumption requires that the inference be made.
>
> Presumptions may also be either rebuttable or irrebuttable. If a presumption is rebuttable, there are three potential ways the presumed fact can be rebutted. First, the accused may be required merely to raise a reasonable

---

[1] (1986), 50 C.R. (3d) 1, 24 C.C.C. (3d) 321 (S.C.C.), at pp. 330-331 (C.C.C.).

doubt as to its existence. Secondly, the accused may have an evidentiary burden to adduce sufficient evidence to bring into question the truth of the presumed fact. Thirdly, the accused may have a legal or persuasive to prove
on a balance of probabilities the non-existence of the presumed fact.

Finally, presumptions are often referred to as either presumptions of law
or presumptions of fact. The latter entail 'frequently recurring examples of
circumstantial evidence' ... while the former involved actual legal rules.

Presumptions are then really aids to assist a court in determining
the issue before it. They are not, in themselves, either evidence or
argument, although they may be based on general experience or
probability, or even on policy and convenience. A few examples
using the categories outlined by Chief Justice Dickson offer
assistance.

Section 354(1) of the *Criminal Code*[2] makes it an offence for
anyone to have in his possession any property knowing that it was
obtained by the commission in Canada of an indictable offence.
To succeed on this charge, the Crown must establish the following: firstly, that the accused had the property in his possession; secondly, that the property was obtained by the commission in Canada
of an offence punishable by indictment (usually stolen); and thirdly,
that the accused knew that it was obtained by the commission in
Canada of indictable offence, in other words, that he knew that
it was stolen.

The doctrine of recent possession, a common law rule, states
that where an accused is found in possession of goods proved to
have been *recently* stolen, the judge or jury, as the case may be,
may infer not only that he had possession of goods knowing them
to have been stolen, but also that he participated in whatever offence
was committed by which the goods were obtained. On the prosecution of the accused, all that the Crown has to establish is that
the goods were found in the possession of the accused and that they
were recently stolen. Common experience tells us that people in possession of goods that were recently stolen or obtained illegally should
have some knowledge of how they were obtained.

The law then casts upon these people a presumption of guilty
knowledge unless, during the course of the trial, an explanation is
offered. The rule is that the judge must tell the jury (or himself
if he is trying the case alone) that they *may*, not that they must,

---

[2] R.S.C. 1985, c. C-46.

in the absence of an explanation that might reasonably be true find the accused guilty.[3] Even if no explanation is offered whatsoever, the judge or jury are entitled to find the accused guilty but are not required to do so.

This is a permissive presumption. It leaves optional the question whether the inference of the presumed fact (that is, guilty knowledge) should be drawn following proof of the basic fact (possession by the accused of goods recently stolen). It does not require the inference to be drawn.

Another example may assist in understanding what is meant by a mandatory presumption. Section 354(2) of the *Code* specifically provides that where an accused is found in possession of a motor vehicle that has the identification number wholly or partially obliterated, two presumptions will arise: the first is that the vehicle was obtained by the commission of an indictable offence; the second is that the accused knew that the vehicle was obtained by the commission of an indictable offence. However, this statutory presumption, unlike the common law doctrine of recent possession, is a mandatory presumption of law because section 354(2) provides that where the basic facts are established (possession of a motor vehicle by the accused with the identification number wholly or partially obliterated), this will amount to "proof" that the accused had the vehicle in his possession *knowing* that it was obtained by the commission of an indictable offence. Unlike a permissive presumption, a mandatory presumption requires the judge or jury to conclude that the presumed fact has been established unless there is evidence to the contrary. It is true that the evidence to the contrary need only raise a reasonable doubt. However, if the accused fails to raise a reasonable doubt, the judge is required to instruct the jury that they *must*, not simply may, convict the accused.[4]

Before leaving this area two important presumptions should be discussed briefly.

---

[3] *Ungaro* (1950), 9 C.R. 328, 96 C.C.C. 245 (S.C.C.).
[4] *Re Boyle* (1983), 5 C.C.C. (3d) 193 (Ont. C.A.).

2. SPECIFIC PRESUMPTIONS

(a) The Presumption of Innocence

The presumption of innocence has been long recognized under the common law. In *Woolmington v. D.P.P.*[5] Viscount Sankey L.C. wrote,

> Throughout the web of the English Criminal Law one golden thread is always to be seen, that is the duty of the prosecution to prove the prisoner's guilt subject to what I have already said as to the defence of insanity and subject also to any statutory exception. If, at the end of and on whole of the case, there is a reasonable doubt, created by the evidence given by either the prosecution or the prisoner..., the prosecution has not made out the case and the prisoner is entitled to an acquittal. No matter what the charge or where the trial, the principle that the prosecution must prove the guilt of the prisoner is part of the common law of England and no attempt to whittle it down can be entertained.

That principle has received international recognition in the *Universal Declaration of Human Rights* adopted December 10, 1948 by the General Assembly of the United Nations and by the International Covenant on Civil and Political Rights, 1966, article 14 (2). It has also been given constitutional guarantee in Canada by section 11(d) of the *Charter Rights and Freedoms*.[6] That section provides,

> 11. Any person charged with an offence has the right
>   (d) to be presumed innocent until proven guilty according to law in a fair and public hearing by an independent and impartial tribunal.

The right simply means that there is no obligation upon an accused to respond either by giving evidence personally or by calling other witnesses. The burden is on the Crown to prove the accused's guilt beyond a reasonable doubt.

---

[5] (1935), A.C. 462 (H.L.), at pp.481-482.
[6] *Canadian Charter of Rights and Freedoms*, Part 1 of the Constitution Act, 1982, being Schedule B to the Canada Act 1982 (U.K.), 1982, c. 11.

(b) The Presumption of No Mental Disorder

Section 16(1) of the *Code* provides that "no person is criminally responsible for an act committed or an omission made while suffering from a mental disorder that rendered the person incapable of appreciating the nature and quality of the act or omission or of knowing that it was wrong." However, section 16(2) goes on to provide that "every person is presumed not to suffer from a mental disorder so as to be exempt from criminal responsibility by virtue of subsection (1), unless the contrary is proved on the balance of probabilities."

Both the Crown and the defence have a right to raise the question of whether the accused is suffering from a mental disorder. However, section 16(3) says that whoever raises it must bear that burden of proof. It has been held that this shift of onus to the accused to prove that he or she is suffering from a mental disorder may be an unconstitutional infringement of an accused's presumption of innocence as guaranteed by section 11(d) of the *Charter* but is saved by section 1 as a reasonable limitation on that presumption.[7]

3. BURDENS OF PROOF

The close relationship between presumptions and burdens of proof often make it difficult to distinguish between the two. It is probably easier to state what the burden of proof is rather than to define it. In a dispute between parties, the burden of proof is the evidentiary burden which the court imposes on one side or the other. The general rule is that the burden of proof lies on the party who asserts the affirmative of the issue or question in dispute. The extent of that burden will vary depending on the nature of the trial.

For example, in a civil trial, where A is suing B for breach of contract, the burden of proof is upon A to establish that breach. In civil cases, the onus is simply on a balance of probabilities. The most vivid example of that onus is the tipping of scales slightly in favour of the person who has the burden. If A tips the scales in his favour, ever so slightly, he wins. If the scales are tipped in favour of B or are evenly balanced, then A loses because he has failed to discharge the burden.

---

[7] *Chaulk* (1991), 2 C.R. (4th) 1, 62 C.C.C. (3d) 193 (S.C.C.).

In a criminal case, the burden is always upon the prosecution and never shifts to the accused. The burden is also more onerous. That burden is to establish the guilt of the accused beyond a reasonable doubt.

4. CONSTITUTIONAL GUARANTEES

As was pointed out earlier, section 11(d) of the *Charter* guarantees every person charged with an offence the right "to be presumed innocent until proven guilty according to law in a fair and public hearing by an independent and impartial tribunal." Since the enactment of that section, there have been a number of cases in Canada attacking presumptions, both permissive and legal, as breaching section 11(d). These presumptions, described as reverse onus provisions, have been attacked on the basis that they have whittled down the presumption of innocence. The position of the Crown in these cases has generally been that these presumptions have been created by statute because there is a close connection between the basic fact and the presumed fact. Unless the presumption is allowed to stand, there will be instances where the Crown may be unable to prove its case. Thus, it is argued that section 1 of the *Charter* protects presumptions as a reasonable limit in a free and democratic society.

In *Downey*,[8] Cory J., delivering the judgment of the majority panel of the Supreme Court of Canada, summarized the principles governing the constitutionality of statutory presumptions:

1. The presumption of innocence is infringed whenever the accused is liable to be convicted despite the existence of a reasonable doubt.
2. If by the provisions of a statutory presumption, an accused is required to prove or disprove on a balance of probabilities either an element of an offence or an excuse, then it contravenes s. 11(d) of the *Charter*. Such a provision would permit a conviction in spite of a reasonable doubt.
3. Even if a rational connection exists between the established fact and the presumed fact, this would be insufficient to make valid a presumption requiring the accused to disprove an element of the offence.

---

[8] (1992), 13 C.R. (4th) 129, 72 C.C.C. (3d) 1 (S.C.C.).

4. Legislation which substitutes proof of one element for proof of an essential element will not infringe the presumption of innocence if, as result of the proof of the substituted element, it would be unreasonable for the trier of fact not to be satisfied beyond a reasonable doubt of the existence of the other element. In other words, a statutory presumption will be valid if proof of the substituted fact leads inexorably to the proof of the other. The statutory presumption will infringe s.11(d) if it requires the trier of fact to convict in spite of a reasonable doubt.

5. A permissive assumption from which a trier of fact may, but not must, draw an inference of guilt will not infringe s. 11(d) of the *Charter*.

6. A provision that might have been intended to play a minor role in providing relief from conviction will nonetheless contravene the *Charter* if the provision (such as the truth of a statement) must be established by the accused.

In *Oakes*,[9] the Supreme Court of Canada set out the test which should be applied in determining whether or not a section of a statute which breached the *Charter* was saved by section 1. One of those considerations was whether the measures adopted were carefully designed to achieve the objective in question. In other words, a presumed fact in a statute could not be saved by section 1 unless it was rationally connected to the basic fact. In the *Oakes* case, the defence argued that section 8 of the *Narcotic Control Act*,[10] which requires an accused found in possession of a narcotic to disprove on a balance of probabilities that he had the narcotic in his possession for the purpose of trafficking, violated section 11(d) of the *Charter* and was not saved by section 1. The Court agreed with the argument. It was held that there was no rational connection between the basic fact of possession and the presumed fact of possession for the purpose of trafficking since the reverse onus clause could give rise to unjustified and erroneous convictions for drug trafficking of persons guilty only of possession of a small quantity of narcotics. Section 8 was held to be unconstitutional as infringing the presumption of innocence in section 11(d).

In *Re Boyle*,[11] discussed earlier, the Court of Appeal of Ontario

---

[9] (1986), 50 C.R. (3d) 1, 24 C.C.C. (3d) 321 (S.C.C.).

[10] R.S.C. 1985, c. N-1.

[11] *Supra*, note 4.

considered the rationality of the connection between the basic fact (possession of a motor vehicle with a wholly or partially obliterated identification number) with the two presumed facts (that the vehicle was obtained by the commission of an indictable offence and that the accused had guilty knowledge) and found the first presumed fact constitutionally valid but not the second. It was held that the only conceivable reason for removing or obliterating a vehicle identification number was to conceal the fact that it had been stolen or had been obtained by the commission of an indictable offence. On the other hand, since the presumption of guilty knowledge was not restricted to persons such as car dealers, who might reasonably be presumed to be knowledgable with respect to the location of vehicle identification numbers and to be alive to the desirability of making an examination to ascertain whether there had been obliteration of such numbers, there was no rational connection between the basic fact and the presumed fact.

10

Particular Problems of Proof

1. JUDICIAL NOTICE

Not every fact in issue need be proved by the introduction of evidence. The law has long recognized that some matters are so notorious they do not require formal proof. As one judge said,

> Courts will take judicial notice of what is considered by reasonable men of that time and place to be indisputable either by resort to common knowledge or to sources of indisputable accuracy easily accessible to men in the situation of members of that court.[1]

This does not mean that the matter can never be disputed. It is nothing more than a *prima facie* recognition of the matter as true without the offering of evidence by the side that asserts it and who would ordinarily be required to prove it. However, the other side is entitled to dispute it if he believes it disputable.[2]

Judicial notice may be taken of the law or of a certain fact. For example, the common law requires the court to take judicial notice of the common law and all public statutes without those statutes being specifically pleaded. Legislative expression of this rule is contained in sections 17 and 18 of the *Canada Evidence Act*.[3] Sections 20 to 27 of the *Act* also provides a method of proving Imperial proclamations, orders in council, treaties, order, warrants,

---

[1] *Bennett* (1971), 15 C.R.N.S. 28, 4 C.C.C. (2d) 55 (N.S. Co. Ct.), per O'Hearn Co. Ct. J., at p. 66 (C.C.C.).

[2] *Zundel* (1987), 56 C.R. (3d) 1, 31 C.C.C. (3d) 97 (Ont. C.A.).

[3] R.S.C. 1985, c. C-5.

etc., as well as those of the Governor General in Council and the lieutenant governor in council of a province, judicial proceedings and official or public documents. In all other cases, the common law requires formal proof.

What constitutes common knowledge of a fact will be judged by reference to that which is common knowledge in the community where and when the issue is being tried, even though it may be unknown elsewhere.[4] For example, a judge sitting in the City of Kitchener may take judicial notice of the fact that Kitchener lies within the Regional Municipality of Waterloo, but not necessarily that a small village lies within the boundaries of the Region.[5] Other examples where judicial notice has been taken are that whisky, beer and wine are intoxicating,[6] that a large screwdriver is an instrument capable of being used for housebreaking[7] and that bridges are publicly owned property.[8] On the other hand, courts are not yet allowed to take judicial notice of a distinctive cultural characteristic in the absence of evidence of that characteristic.[9]

Although a judge is entitled to take judicial notice of a fact, he is not necessarily required to do so even if it is generally known and accepted. A judge is entitled to refuse to take judicial notice of a fact that is essential to the Crown's case where to do so would gravely prejudice the case for the defence.[10]

2. IDENTITY

It has been long recognized and accepted by the courts that identification based on personal impressions, that is human observation and recollections, is notoriously unreliable. When a witness says "that is the man" without pointing out any distinctive features which single him out from others, that kind of identification will be given little weight or value. Why? The reason is because of the possibility of honest error.[11]

---

[4] *Potts* (1982), 26 C.R. (3d) 252, 66 C.C.C. (2d) 219 (Ont. C.A.), leave to appeal refused (1982), 66 C.C.C. (2d) 219n (S.C.C.).
[5] *Eagles* (1976), 31 C.C.C. (2d) 417 (Ont. H.C.).
[6] *Moxley* (1928), 50 C.C.C. 408 (Man. C.A.).
[7] *Robert*, [1969] 3 C.C.C. 165 (B.C. C.A.).
[8] *Rese*, 2 C.R.N.S. 99, [1968] 1 C.C.C. 363 (Ont. C.A.).
[9] *W. (S.)* (1991), 6 C.R. (4th) 373 (Ont. C.A.).
[10] *Zundel, supra,* note 2.
[11] *Sutton* (1970), 9 C.R.N.S. 45, [1970] 3 C.C.C. 152 (Ont. C.A.); *Spatola* (1970), 10 C.R.N.S. 143, [1970] 4 C.C.C. 241 (Ont. C.A.).

The most common example of identification evidence being considered valueless is where a witness identifies the accused for the first time while the accused is sitting in the prisoner's dock. Another is where a witness is asked to look at the accused to see if he can recognize him as the person who committed the offence. Such identification has been called "unfair and unjust".[12] In *Browne*[13] the British Columbia Court of Appeal described that kind of identification as,

> ...valueless in the sense that it is dangerous for a Court to act upon it in any respect. Its inherent tendencies towards honest mistake and self-deception are so pervasive that they destroy any value that could otherwise attach to it in a lesser role of 'some evidence'.

The trier will thus be asked to look at other evidence which supports that identification before a finding of guilt may be made. For example, were there any distinguishing features, either physical, or in speech, or dress which singled out that person from others? Unless there is some unusual or distinguishing feature which supports or confirms the initial identification, the trial judge must warn the jury (and himself where he sit alone) that a conviction based on such evidence is generally unsafe.

The usual practice where identity is in issue is for the police to show the witness a series of photographs, called a photo-lineup, and ask the witness whether "anyone looks familiar to him." Alternatively, if a suspect is believed to have committed the offence, the police may conduct a lineup of individuals (an identification parade) including the suspect and ask the witness whether he can identify anyone. In *Goldhar*,[14] the Ontario Court of Appeal stressed that when conducting the identification parade, two matters should be clearly kept in mind.

> First, it should appear that there is nothing whatever done to indicate to the witness the person in the line-up who is suspected by the police, either by showing the photograph or by description, or an indication of the position in the line-up. In the second place, it should appear that the selection of the other persons to form the line-up has been fairly so that the suspect

---

12 *Smierciak* (1946), 2 C.R. 434, 87 C.C.C. 175 (Ont. C.A.), at p. 177.
13 (1951), 99 C.C.C. 141 (B.C. C.A.), at pp. 149-150.
14 (1941), 76 C.C.C. 270 (Ont. C.A.), at pp. 271-272.

will not be conspicuously different from all the others in age or build, colour or complexion or costume or in any other particular.

In such instance, the court must be satisfied that the identification of the accused by the witness out of a series of photographs or out of a lineup was not induced by suggestion.

A witness who is giving testimony will be routinely asked by the prosecutor if he sees the accused in court and will be asked to point him out. If this is the first opportunity for the witness to identify the accused in the dock or if the witness made a prior identification that was induced by suggestion rendering the identification in court worthless, does the trial judge have the right either at common law or under the *Charter of Rights and Freedoms*[15] as a breach of section 7 (fundamental justice) or section 11(d) (presumption of innocence) to exclude the identification evidence altogether? That issue appears to have been first addressed by the Supreme Court of Canada in *Mezzo*,[16] a rape trial. There the trial judge had directed a verdict of acquittal because the identification procedures carried out by the police had been flawed casting serious doubt on the accuracy and reliability of the complainant's identification of the accused as her attacker. Although the Court ordered a new trial on the basis that there was some evidence that should have been left to the jury with a proper charge by the trial judge, Madame Justice Wilson in a separate concurring decision (concurred in by Chief Justice Dickson) suggested that the proper procedure to consider improprieties was by way of a motion to exclude the evidence either under a trial judge's common law discretion to exclude prejudicial evidence having little or no probative value or, under section 24 of the *Charter*. Similar views appear to have been adopted by the Courts of Appeal of British Columbia in *Thomas*[17] and *Fraser*[18] and Ontario in *D'Amico*,[19] although in none of those cases was the accused successful.

---

[15] *Canadian Charter of Rights and Freedoms*, Part 1 of the Constitution Act, 1982, being Schedule B to the Canada Act 1982 (U.K.), 1982, c. 11.

[16] (1986), 52 C.R. (3d) 113, 27 C.C.C. (3d) 97 (S.C.C.).

[17] (1993), 24 C.R. (4th) 249 (B.C. C.A.).

[18] (1993), 80 C.C.C. (3d) 539 (B.C. C.A.).

[19] (1993), 16 O.R. (3d) 125 (C.A.).

3. INTENT

As was pointed out in Chapter 1, one of the issues that the Crown must prove is that the accused intended to commit the prohibited act. The problem, however, is that what goes on in a person's mind is often difficult, if not impossible, to ascertain. But the courts have found no difficulty in making that determination. As Bowen L.J. said in *Edgington v. Fitzmaurice*,[20]

> ...the state of a man's mind is as much a fact as the state of his digestion. It is true that is very difficult to prove what the state of a man's mind at a particular time is, but if it can be ascertained it is as much a fact as anything else...

Some of the ways that a person's intent can be proved are by what he says or admits to others, or what he does. The most common method, however, is by what is known as the presumption of intent. This presumption says that a man is presumed to have intended the natural consequences of his acts. In other words, if X shoots his gun at Y, it is open for the court to draw the inference that X did so intending to kill or injure Y.

Such a presumption, however, is not considered to be a presumption of law, merely one of good common sense. As Roach J.A. pointed out in *Giannotti*,[21]

> ...a man is usually able to foresee what are the natural consequences of his acts, so it is, as a rule, reasonable to infer that he did foresee them and intend them. But, while that is an inference which may be drawn, it is not one which must be drawn. If on all the facts of the case it is not the correct inference, then it should not be drawn.

4. CONSPIRACY

As was pointed out in Chapter 3, although what one accused says about his co-accused is not evidence of the co-accused's guilt, there is an exception to that rule where an accused is charged with conspiracy. Acts and declarations of one conspirator in furtherance

---

[20] (1885), 29 Ch. D. 459, at p. 483.
[21] (1956), 23 C.R. 259, 115 C.C.C. 203 (Ont. C.A.), at p. 213 (C.C.C.).

of the common design may be given in evidence against all the conspirators.[22] But before such evidence may be considered, the trier must first be satisfied that the accused is *probably* a member of the conspiracy by evidence directly admissible against him without relying upon the hearsay exception. Once the trier is satisfied as to this *probability*, then the trier is entitled to consider the acts and declarations of co-conspirators on the final issue of whether the Crown has proven the guilt of the accused *beyond a reasonable doubt*.[23]

One might assume that because of this exception, conspiracy cases create a two stage trial, the first involving evidence directly proving membership of the accused in the conspiracy and a determination by the trier of the probability of that membership, and then a second where hearsay evidence is allowed of the acts and declarations of co-conspirators. In *Carter*,[24] it was held that this was not necessary because "the exigencies of the trial would make a chronological separation of the evidence impossible". It was only necessary for the trial judge to charge the jury that they were to sift through the evidence and follow this procedure:

1. Consider whether on all the evidence, they are satisfied beyond a reasonable doubt that the conspiracy charged existed;
2. If they are so satisfied, they must decide whether, on the evidence directly admissible against the accused, a probability is raised that he was a member of the conspiracy;
3. Only if they conclude that there is such evidence can they apply the hearsay exception in determining whether guilt has been shown beyond a reasonable doubt.

---

[22] *Koufis* (1941), 76 C.C.C. 161 (S.C.C.).
[23] *Carter* (1982), 31 C.R. (3d) 97, 67 C.C.C. (2d) 568 (S.C.C.).
[24] *Ibid.*, at 105 (C.R.).

Index